ONE STONE FOR
TIBET

Janice Harvey

Janice Harvey lives with her two sons in the most isolated capital city in the world – Perth, Western Australia.

ISBN No. 0-646-35232-6
First Edition April1998

Copyright © Janice Harvey 1998
Photography Copyright © Irene Smith 1998

Printed and bound in Australia by the Sands Print Group
Designed by Steve Davis
Set in Baskerville and Optima
Artwork and Pre-Press by Alken Colour Media

Published by
Awareness Publications
Post Office Box 967, Nedlands
Western Australia 6909

Cover illustration:
The Knot of Eternity represents the entwined, never ending passage of harmony and love. It is seen throughout Tibet.

Impressions and Images

of Tibet

To Graham

With my heartfelt
Thanks for your support,

Grace Harvey
1998

Dedicated to

Gary-la

*A man with many titles
but no need to use them*

*"Images of Tibet"
Photographed by*

Irene-la

*(Tibetans use "la" at the end of a name as an honorific.
It denotes friendly respect or endearment. For instance,
Shangri-la meant that the idea of the place of Shangri
was very special in the author's heart.)*

One Stone for Tibet

CONTENTS

Foreword

1	David and Goliath	1
2	China's Shame	7
3	True Tibetans	13
4	Exile	25
5	Waiting for His Holiness	27
6	Misinformation	35
7	The Peaceful Path	43
8	Lhasa Today	49
9	Homes of a Humble Man	55
10	The Potala	63
11	The Barkhor	79
12	Tashi Tsering	89
13	Nuclear Cataclysm	93

14	Farewell Yamdrok-tso	99
15	Milarepa	109
16	Great Monasteries	119
17	Four Directions	129
18	Panchen Lama	133
19	Moving Along	141
20	Sky Burial	147
21	Former Glory	151
22	Landslides	157
23	Welcome and Farewell	165
	Epilogue	173

One Stone for Tibet

FOREWORD

So many of us in the western world are fascinated by Tibet. We were tantalised in our youth with stories of Shangri-la, mystified by the self sufficiency of the Tibetans and longing to know more about this almost inaccessible land at the top of the world. Sadly, very few curious travellers were privileged to experience the splendour of Tibet prior to the Chinese tightening the borders for over twenty years from 1959 to 1981.

The invasive Chinese presence has now been in Tibet for nigh onto fifty years. As we draw near to the close of this century most of the world's civilised nations carry a certain guilt about the oppression in modern Tibet. However, guilt does not absolve the atrocities nor resolve the issue. In 1997, in an attempt to better understand the situation, Janice Harvey spent a month in Tibet with a group of fellow travellers. "One Stone for Tibet" is drawn from her observations on that tour.

Chapter One
DAVID AND GOLIATH

"Pasang-la, Pasang-la! Pull over here. Stop the coach."

Pasang-la was our Tibetan driver and he pulled onto the verge with a bemused look on his face. He was obviously accustomed to European tour group leaders making strange requests at a moments notice.

We all perked up to see what new aspect of Tibet was about to reveal itself.

We were travelling on the sealed road into Lhasa, the capital city of this vast and mystical land. The wide and sparkling Brahmaputra, the river with a name like a magic spell, was on our right. A few hundred yards to the left were the barren hills which lined the valley. It

One Stone for Tibet

was a scene from a child's painting. A strip of bright blue sky above brown hills. A patch of green dotted with sheep and the grey road running next to the water's edge.

The never ending panorama of brown hills held us fascinated because of the precarious texture of their surfaces. Almost all the hillsides and mountain slopes in Tibet are covered with a loose slate like shingle, which slips and slides and causes many sudden landfalls. We were in an untamed land where the powers of nature still held sway.

Between the road and the hills a couple of boys were herding sheep and yaks. Our guide beckoned to one of the boys and as he made his way over to the coach we were all asked to get out of the bus and stand on the riverbank.

We were soon to gasp in wonder as this mere dot of a boy showed us his skill with a slingshot. As he whirled the stones above his head he aimed them out into the river. Some of them flew so far we lost sight of them. Others were aimed with the intention of truly impressing us and we heard sharp cracks as they hit the water at just the right angle and then bounced off like the bombs in the Dambusters. Our young friend was delighted to have an audience and even happier when our guide gave him a handful of sweets for his demonstration.

With hours to fill in as he herded his flocks, and not much in the way of entertainment, this young fellow had spent his time mastering this ancient skill.

We were taken back in time as we stood in this quiet, empty valley. It was the perfect setting in which to recall the Bible story of David and Goliath. The story came alive for us. No wonder tiny David managed to slay the massive giant Goliath. We had just watched a marksman at work.

Thousands of years ago one young lad named David killed a

giant and with one stone changed the course of history. Modern Tibet is a country which needs a dynamic change in its history to restore the peace which once prevailed in this land.

An old tune we had sung as children in Sunday School began buzzing through my head.

> *"Only a boy named David*
> *Only a babbling brook*
> *Only a boy named David*
> *And one little stone he took*
> *And one little stone went in the sling*
> *And the sling went round and round*
> *And one little stone went in the sling*
> *And the sling went round and round*
> *And round and round*
> *And round and round*
> *And round and round and round*
> *And one little stone flew through the air*
> *Whirrrrrrrrrrrrrrrrrrrrr*
> *And the giant came tumbling down"*

There is so little hope for Tibet at the moment and yet this tune kept bringing me back to David and Goliath. Maybe the present Dalai Lama is the modern David. Perhaps his allegorical weapon in his stance for Tibet is the example he shows to all of us in his serene acceptance that there is always a gentle path. His message has certainly 'hit the world between the eyes' with its focused intensity on one word - his "One Stone for Tibet" is PEACE.

Ever so many people criticised the Dalai Lama when he chose the path of non-aggression against the Chinese invaders. He 'walked his talk' and did not bow to pressure. I doubt if even the Dalai Lama himself knew what history would reveal decades after his escape but he stayed true to his beliefs and now a most interesting scenario has unravelled.

After nearly forty years in exile His Holiness has proven to us all the wisdom of the old saying "The Years Teach Much Which The Days Never See". The Chinese can try every tactic and manoeuvre for self-justification of their actions but the truth, which has been revealed over time, unveils their motives.

There is absolutely no way the Chinese can accuse the Dalai Lama of aggression which could have incited their takeover because he is living proof of his non-violent stance. Thankfully many of the 'humane' movers and shakers in this world acknowledged that fact when the Dalai Lama was awarded the Nobel Peace Prize in 1989. Now the world media is aware of the charisma of His Holiness. This humble man has raised the consciousness of the world through simply 'being' himself.

Chapter Two
CHINA'S SHAME

One of the Chinese ploys in their political game is to create uncertainty and to accuse all and sundry of offences which are often totally fabricated. When they first invaded Tibet their propaganda sent a message to the world that they were liberating the oppressed Tibetan people. We were assured the Tibetans welcomed the Chinese and that their impoverished lives would now be enriched by communist ways.

There were many in the western world who 'swallowed' this propaganda as it gave them a way out of needing to help the Tibetans. Their thought patterns ran along these lines:

- Maybe the Chinese are right and the Tibetans will welcome modern living conditions.
- Let's face it, the Tibetans are 'weird' because they have always been so self-contained.
- Perhaps the Chinese will bring them into this century!

This simplistic attitude allowed the greatest nations on this planet to feign indifference to the Tibetan cause. The western world wanted to believe the Chinese were altruistic and genuinely liberating the Tibetans. Even today some extremely high ranking political figures still hold this simplistic view.

I find it hard to believe that Tibetans would not have had the capacity to integrate modern ideas if left alone. After all, the

Dalai Lama himself has an exceedingly inquisitive mind and loved dabbling with electronic gadgets and cars well before he left Lhasa. Educated Tibetans have always been noted for their scholarship as well as their quest for knowledge and it is an affront to pretend they were a backward country. If anything, their belief system had led to an evolved society where materialism was not the ultimate goal. This is a concept which many westerners are now seeking in a bid to find peace in a bustling world.

The chink in the armour of the Chinese government is in the proof of the reality. No matter how hard the Chinese protest their innocence and desire to 'liberate' the Tibetans, the facts speak more loudly.

- If you want to set someone free you do not then resort to torture, destruction and continued violence against those whom you are trying to save.
- If the Chinese truly believe communism is the pathway to happiness, their methods of 'converting' the Tibetans are abhorrent to any fair minded person.

Instead of helping the Tibetans, the Chinese have attempted to destroy the culture through decimating the monastic system. Sadly, to the Chinese iconoclasts way of thinking, this also meant destroying those who lived within this system. Probably the most distressing realisation of my entire trip to Tibet was the day a clear truth hit me:

"My generation was missing from the monasteries and nunneries!"

Admittedly there are a token few elderly folk in each monastery but basically the forty to seventy year olds have been purged. Some may still be in jail or back on road gangs or working the fields, but most of them are dead – killed by the Chinese invaders.

This sickening thought gave me a small insight into the Nazi death camps. For the free world these camps were our lesson. We learn from history and millions vowed that the world had learned the lesson and learned it well. We believed this grotesque behaviour would never blacken our planet again. If ever vile atrocities such as those perpetrated in the Nazi camps rose again we were confident they would be exposed and eradicated. Even as we voiced our opinions and placed confidence in our leaders to ensure they guarded our beliefs, the Tibetans were being savagely culled.

If the Chinese were true 'liberationists' they would move out of Tibet and acknowledge that the Tibetans are perfectly capable of self government. Sadly, the Chinese see Tibet as the source of untold mineral wealth and as a nuclear waste dump. Tibet, poised on 'top of the world' is the source of seven of Asia's great river systems. The Chinese only need to make one major nuclear mistake and they have the ability to destroy much of the Asian eco-system. The pacifist Tibetans were the perfect 'guardians' of the top of the world because they had no intention of abusing their land with tools of destruction.

Then again, maybe the "One Stone for Tibet" is a young man or woman growing up in modern day China. A few of Tibets most beautiful buildings were saved after intervention from one or two Chinese leaders with more foresight than the rest. If only one world leader emerges from China with compassion and understanding nearing that of the Dalai Lama, the future of Tibet can again be one of peace.

Interestingly, the Dalai Lama himself is so lacking in ego that he has always been willing to co-operate in a peaceful resolution for Tibet. He does not seek political power as a condition of his return to his country. He is the first to acknowledge that times have changed and his people may prefer an elected government. In 1992 His Holiness issued a statement that when Tibet regains its independence he is willing to live as a private citizen. The Dalai Lama has even proposed peace plans to China which seek friendship and co-operation and, in the main, seek the transformation of Tibet into a recognised zone of peace and neutrality once more. However, he cannot return to Tibet while the present leaders in China maintain their biased and aggressive political stance.

At the moment, over 100,000 Tibetans, most of whom retain a deep desire to return home, are living in exile. The countries which harbour them deserve our gratitude. India, Nepal, Bhutan, Switzerland, Germany, Spain, England, Canada, the USA, Australia and New Zealand are amongst the nations which have been prepared to let the Tibetans stay until they can repatriate.

A tiny white butterfly, with its quivering gossamer wings, rested trustingly beside me today. It was no bigger than my smallest fingernail and yet it was perfect in every detail. As I gazed in wonder at its fragile beauty my mind drifted into thoughts of the miracle of life on our planet.

And then it came to me. The realisation that in the early half of this century we had a nation of people in our midst who were truly endeavouring to live in harmony with nature and with one another and the rest of the world. Tibetans never willingly harm another living creature. The essence of their culture is gentleness towards anything which the creator has chosen to put on this earth and they go the extra mile in their efforts to live by this creed of care for the wellbeing of all. Their example is a way which we only hold as a dream for our children - a world where every thing has a reason to be and because of this it has a validity and a place in the universal plan. In an appalling twist of fate the Tibetans now have to dream along with us because their land where 'dreams come true' has been tarnished.

In Heinrich Harrer's book "Return to Tibet" one of his saddest recollections was that Tibet no longer overflowed with flowers. He said the Tibetans grew flowers anywhere and everywhere and their abundance was an innate part of the texture, aroma and colour of the country. He was shattered by the lack of beauty when he returned to Tibet in 1982. Fifteen years after his journey it saddens me to say that the missing flowers are an ongoing confirmation of the bleakness of the Chinese regime. What an indictment. To invade a land of beauty and enshroud it in a pall of dingy grey.

Very few, except the Tibetan Oracles, envisaged the effects of the invasion from the North. Most of the incredible events which have changed the path of history on our planet Earth were not predicted. One battle lost or won, one President dead or alive, one explorer in a new frontier, a Mother Theresa in the slums or a movie star with a 'cause', one song by Elton John, one interview with Oprah, athletes who inspire, poets, scholars, people with vendettas or others with a desire for peace - each one of us has the capacity to speak or act and affect the whole. And once in a while, one person turns the key to a monumental change.

Chapter Three
TRUE TIBETANS

In 1933 the progressive Thirteenth Dalai Lama died. He had spent much of his life planning a system of reforms for his people in the areas of political, social and economic structures. He felt that the Tibetan system, although peaceful, was still too feudal and his desire was to gently introduce change.

After his death the people waited patiently for change knowing that when the Fourteenth Dalai Lama was found, and came of age, he would continue the work of his predecessor. The Tibetans followed their age old procedure for finding the next Dalai Lama and finally came to the child who recognised the belongings of the Thirteenth ruler. The Fourteenth Dalai Lama was discovered when he was two, enthroned when he was four and assumed full authority in 1950 when he was fifteen.

The future of the world changed dramatically in 1949 when the Chinese communists defeated the Chinese Nationalist Party and created the People's Republic of China. Almost immediately, the Chinese announced their intention of annexing Tibet. The Tibetan Foreign Office sent a plea to the United Nations on the understanding that the U.N. has "decided to stop aggression wherever it takes place". It fell on deaf ears.

In 1950 the Chinese decided to exercise their might and make their presence a force to be reckoned with in Tibet and by

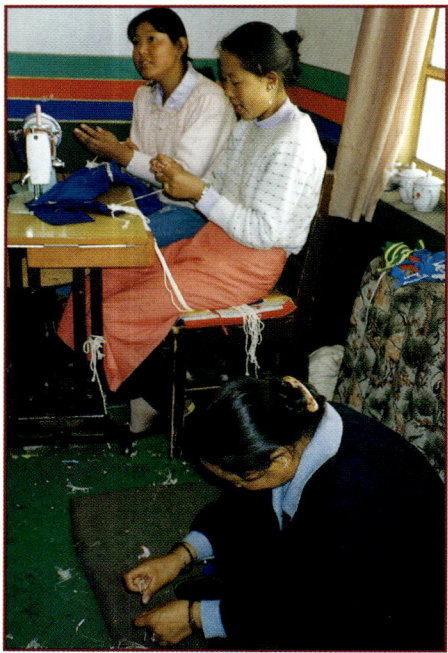

September 1951 the troops marched into Lhasa, the capital city. People in Lhasa were horrified at the sight of the troops, and the aggressive attitude of the soldiers, but it was only a foretaste of what was to come. From that day they have never been able to call their country their own.

The Chinese believed this mysterious nation of self-contained people "belonged" to them and they wanted the rest of the world to acknowledge this fact.

In reality the Tibetans look more like their Mongolian neighbours from whom they are believed to have descended. Their facial features are not what we westerners would perceive as typically Chinese. In addition to this, the Tibetan mannerisms are unique to their race. They have what are commonly

True Tibetans

referred to as laughing eyes and an aura of contentment which has even remained after decades of ghastly torture of their citizens. The Tibetan people maintain the most incredible "eye contact" I have experienced. They really look at you when you speak and make you feel as though your words are important to them. They listen closely and react spontaneously, often bursting into laughter if there is any comical nuance in your words. Sorrel Wilby, the Australian woman who trekked across Tibet after cycling around the rest of Asia, commented on this unique quality which the Tibetans have to make you feel warm and included.

In our modern world we often do not even hear what our children or workmates say to us. We spin around with many thoughts running through our heads at the same time. We often miss key words which would tell us how those around us are feeling. It is almost a treat experiencing someone's "undivided attention".

Somehow, in Tibet they either have more time to listen or it is an innate part of their culture. I cannot remember one instance of a Tibetan failing to respond to a greeting. Even women in Lhasa who carry their babies on their backs and spend their days begging from tourists, break into giggles of glee if they see something funny. Their joyful personalities are always waiting to erupt to the surface like bubbles of energy. The Tibetans would be the first to tell you they are not "saints" but many of them give you a strange feeling that if they wished they could wiggle their nose and levitate in front of you just for the fun of it.

Even a gentle woman we met, whose husband had died after the Chinese hammered nails into his head, greeted us with warmth and genuine care. By rights, the Tibetans should be careworn and depressed after nearly fifty years of Chinese annexation, but they retain their natural exuberance. Maybe this serenity can be attributed in part to the Buddhist outlook on life. Buddhists believe suffering is part of our journey and the simple acceptance of this fact, instead of raging against it, must have some effect on their outlook.

A Buddhist path is a steady journey towards Nirvana which is travelled within one's own mind. There is no Buddhist deity of judgement but the Tibetans have merged a lot of their ancient gods from the times before Buddhism into a rattling good religion with lots of ceremonies and pomp and circumstance.

By tradition Tibetan families happily accepted the fact that their sons and daughters could become monks or nuns. Even though the community financially supported these vocations there was little resentment. As children of the people the monks and nuns belonged to everyone and formed an integral part of the fantastic cultural life of Tibet. At least, this was the norm until the second half of this century when the Chinese invaders felt it was their "duty" to abolish Buddhism.

If only the Chinese had studied the philosophies behind this so called religion they would have found that Buddhism encourages you to find your own "middle-path" and is the least fanatical of world religions. Buddhism does not encourage you to give your power to a godhead and yet it still acknowledges other realms. Buddhist statues essentially exist only as reminders of the concepts of the belief system. In a society where not everyone could read and write the statues were indicative of the pathways of suffering, compassion and enlightenment and also played a large part in the ceremony and pageantry which are an innate part of most ancient cultures.

The Buddhist statue with one thousand arms may appear strange to westerners. However, when you move closer you can see that in the palm of each of the one thousand hands is an eye of compassion. Many wall hangings in Tibet have a sword in the centre. However, this sword is the sword of knowledge, not of aggression.

The Chinese determined that the concept of Buddhism should lose its power without realising that Tibetans nurtured each other in such a way that they were true communists. In the same way that the Australian Aboriginal and American Indian people had integrated societies where everyone carried responsibility for everybody as part of the whole, so did the Tibetans.

In fact, modern communist nations do more to divide the people than to encourage them to share. Once the Chinese tried to implement their ideas of communes Tibetans faced their first major famines. They had always stored grain in case of drought and emergency. However, the communists take any spare grain from the communities and leave nothing for times of crisis. The communists also dictate which crops they think the Tibetans should grow and for many years made the farmers plant wheat instead of the traditional barley. It is only after decades of trouble that they have finally realised that the Tibetans knew more about the local terrain than they did.

A similar invasion which interrupted the cycle of life happened to the Incan farmers in South America when the Spanish invaded their lands. Their huge hillside storage granaries were soon looted to feed soldiers and there was nothing set aside for later. It is a simplistic statement but the introduction of military forces into any nation places a strain on local food supplies. Soldiers only consume, they do not replenish and it is an easy matter to throw a finely balanced economy out of kilter.

World Health Authorities have found that the Tibetans lived efficient self-contained lives within the harsh restrictions of their environment. They built their houses of stone, mud bricks and timber in a manner which created superb insulation. They channelled water for hygienic drainage systems. Since the Chinese have tried to alter the crop cycles and house people in concrete flats with no running water there are more avenues for

an increase in illnesses. There have always been problems with altitude sicknesses which affect the lungs of young children. However, when they are rugged up against the cold and fed properly the potential for many illnesses can ease.

Most Tibetans in the countryside used to live in a paradise on earth. Their fields were in the fertile valleys and they lived in communal clusters of houses which constituted small villages. Architecturally the houses are very interesting.

The walls are thicker at the bottom in the manner of Inca designs. Most homes are built around a central courtyard. Stables are on the ground floor with living quarters above. The kitchen is the hub of the home and tsampa (a ground and roasted barley meal) and yak butter tea is always on hand. Strangely enough, nowadays, with many of the women folk in the fields, the ever ready  tea is kept in large thermos flasks. Most houses have a dog and cat and chickens, goats, sheep and a cow or two. Elderly relatives are still part of the communities.

Until the first half of the Twentieth Century the women, children and domestic animals lived in harmony and basically the men tended the fields and the women pitched in with the outdoor work if they had the time. Once the communists took

over the women were made to work in the fields and nowadays the smaller children and babies are minded by their siblings. All over Tibet you can see wee little girls with babies strapped on their backs. Some of these children only look six or seven. The little ones are rugged up but they all have their cheeky bare bottoms exposed to the cold, probably because it saves on diapers if they can just be off-loaded in a field when nature calls.

Many changes have occurred in Tibet since the Chinese takeover. One, which is having a profound effect, is the Chinese policy of one child per family. In a country with a fairly high mortality rate this edict causes many problems. If your only child happens to die you have no-one to tend to family needs or care for you in your old age. No longer can families happily accept a child's decision to enter a monastery as that generally precludes the option of grandchildren. However, certain monks in Tibet have always been allowed to marry and raise families. It is only the highest orders, such as the Yellow Hats, who vow to be celibate.

It is very difficult for those of us in the west to perceive a society where such a pedantic rule as the one-child policy even exists, let alone one where it is adhered to. It is a fact that the Chinese police this policy in a very strict manner throughout all their lands. Many abortions are necessitated by the state, rather than the desire of the parents. As a result of this policy it is now acknowledged that many people are testing for the sex of their unborn child. Girls are culled relentlessly as boys are viewed as the preferred option. Throughout China the ratio of boys to girls is now sixty percent male to forty percent female. This imbalance is already causing men to marry women from outside their culture and many are seeking wives in Vietnam.

It is hard to predict an outcome of the one child policy. I know people who swear it will result in a nation of spoilt, selfish monsters. This hypothesis may not prove true. There are millions of successful and well adjusted 'only' children in all societies. We must hope that these cherished children in China will become wonderful citizens of the world because they have known the undivided love of their parents.

One Stone for Tibet

The XIV Dalai Lama

Chapter Four
EXILE

For nearly ten years, from the time when Mao Zedong and his new regime of communists began to rule China, the rest of the world dithered and paid lip service to the fact that the Chinese probably should not be in Tibet. Initially it would have been really easy to keep the invaders out because there are so few access routes to Lhasa. However, students of Tibetan history know the story of the hope held by many of the Tibetans for a peaceful resolution to the Chinese occupation. There would have been very few people in Tibet who would have grasped the concept of the aggression which was about to come from the Chinese. Concerned people around the world have been stunned by the atrocities which have been perpetrated.

Once the Chinese controlled the main entry routes and forced the building of the airport, the country was theirs. Too bad if the Khampa warriors of Eastern Tibet were willing to fight to the death. Once the capital was under Chinese rule the battle was over.

Despite this invasion the Dalai Lama was still residing in Lhasa. He was a peaceful man who did not seek conflict. In fact, he was so conciliatory that his own people began to fear the Chinese would whisk him away and they would lose their revered leader. The local people were justified in their fears and communicated to one another by word of mouth until almost every citizen in the immediate area of Lhasa was aware of what was happening.

In 1959 the people of Lhasa decided to act. They surrounded the Norbulingka, the Summer Palace, because they feared the Chinese may try to take the Dalai Lama away within the next few days. The Chinese had issued an invitation to the Dalai Lama and had specifically requested he attend without his entourage.

The situation grew increasingly tense and one night the Dalai Lama's advisers decided it was time for him to escape into exile. After consulting the Oracle and saying his last prayers in his favourite home, Tenzin Gyatso, the XIV Dalai Lama of Tibet, prepared to leave his country. His Holiness put away his glasses, dressed in trousers and a long black coat and held a rifle over his shoulder. He walked out of the Norbulingka gate beside the Head Bodyguard who simply told the waiting throng he was conducting a routine inspection. By an act of destiny a miraculous dust storm blew up the valley at the opportune time and it was several days before the Chinese realised His Holiness was well and truly gone.

The Tibetans were delighted to know that their leader had escaped safely but the news marked the beginning of an out and out attack against any Tibetans the Chinese perceived as dissenters. Within a year 87,000 were dead at the hands of the soldiers, monasteries were razed, monks and nuns were tortured, men between 16 and 60 were rounded up and sent away to camps in China and the fabric of Tibetan life was destroyed. From 1959 until 1981 no westerner lived in Tibet and the Chinese were free to carry out their purges and atrocities.

Chapter Five
WAITING FOR HIS HOLINESS

In the 1950's Tibet had over 6,000 active monasteries and nunneries. Many of these monasteries housed thousands of monks. The monasteries were the hub of Tibetan life. Fantastic festivals and rituals were performed for both the monks and the people. The monasteries housed magnificent artworks and ceremonial occasions were brilliantly colourful spectacles. Huge images of Buddha called thankas would be rolled down the facade of the Potala and the other monasteries as a sign of harmony and rejoicing. The legendary Shangri-la was almost a reality.

Once the Chinese invaded they began to destroy the monasteries. Entire hillsides are laid bare where centuries old buildings once stood proudly. All over Tibet there are ruins which look similar to the few remaining stones of King Arthur's legendary castle at Tintagel in England. Sadly these ruins are the result of wanton destruction carried out in the last half of this century. When the Chinese ran out of energy to destroy the vast numbers of buildings they forced the Tibetans to destroy their own monuments. Priceless libraries and artefacts have gone forever in the wake of this destructive force.

Nowadays it would be doubtful if even 1,000 monasteries are still standing and the ranks of monks are totally decimated. It really seems as though one of the few reasons the Chinese left any monasteries at all is because they hadn't quite finished destroying everything when they began to listen to world opinion. This same world opinion indicated that people were

fascinated by Tibet and that interest leads to tourism which is a huge money spinner. Tourism without any sites would be rather bland.

So, after decades of decimation we now see some monasteries being restored. However, do not be drawn into the net without being aware. Although many monasteries are reopened to tourists there are some significant changes. Firstly, when is a monk not a monk? No longer can you know who is a true monk and who is a planted informer. Freedom of speech simply does not exist.

Often a Tibetan will sidle up to you and discreetly ask "Dalai Lama picture?"

Everyday Tibetans would give anything for such a picture but no tourist in their right mind would consider even carrying such a thing. If a tourist was reported to be handing out a picture of

His Holiness, he would be escorted out of Tibet, and the rest of his tour group with him. If a Tibetan was caught with the photo he would be liable for jail or torture. This is not an area to be handled lightly.

At one nunnery a sweet faced young nun walked beside me whispering requests for such a photo. Apart from the fact that none of us dared to carry such an incriminating item I really had no idea if she was genuine or a "plant". I would certainly not have been prepared to take the chance of finding out.

It is also worth noting that tourist permits are only meant to be issued for group travellers. This prerequisite enables the authorities to have a fair idea where most tourists are at a given time. It is extremely difficult to slip away and probe into any non-public access area.

Evidence of the change in culture is a daily occurrence in modern Tibet. Tour guides are proud to show visitors the sites including the nunneries and monasteries. However, tourist's needs are secondary to the mission of communist rulers. You cannot simply be welcomed into places of worship at any time. Rather, your guides go ahead to see if it is convenient to visit or if 'lessons' are taking place. 'Lessons' are indoctrination sessions which are held for the 'benefit' of all monks and nuns. These lessons, conducted by Chinese officials can occur at any time. Because of these intrusions into monastic life our group twice missed seeing the famous debating sessions at Sera Monastery.

One day whilst visiting an obscure nunnery we were party to an incredible experience. We had finally managed to find an opportune time to visit and were privileged to be invited into a hall where many nuns were chanting in unison. Immediately two of the nuns rose and placed maroon cushions on extra platforms at the rear of the room so we could watch their ceremony in comfort. Listening to their sonorous lilting voices

Waiting For His Holiness

was a moving experience and we were so grateful to be part of it.

Because of the purges of the nunneries most of the nuns are girls aged from their teens to early twenties. They peeked mischievously at us around the folds of their maroon robes and with their shaven heads they looked very like a roomful of young monks. Probably the most evident difference at first glance was that the room we were in was spotless, whereas some of the monasteries looked liked a 'mob of blokes' were in residence.

The nuns had a five minute rest break in their chanting and many of them scattered off to stretch their legs. As they moved back into the room they nodded and smiled and made us feel really welcome. Tea was poured from large thermos flasks and more giggles were exchanged as they 'sussed out' our western dress and our abundance of photographic equipment. Not only did we come in all shapes and sizes, so did our 'gear'.

After another ten minutes or so of listening to the mellifluous tones of the chanting one of the elderly nuns called another break. She indicated that they would be happy to chat with us. This communication continued for several minutes with some humorous results.

Then I asked if any of the older nuns had been privileged to meet His Holiness. One of them commenced her reply by saying His Holiness had visited her village when she was a child. Then she began to speak of the longing they all felt in their hearts for the day when the Dalai Lama could return to them.

A strange stillness fell over the room and we all found ourselves turning towards an elderly nun who was obviously trying to share her narrative with us. Her words began to tumble out in a torrent of emotion.

She was telling us of the torture the nuns in her community had suffered at the hands of the Chinese. One by one the nuns in front of us began to weep as the story unravelled. Soon every person in the room was caught up in the sorrow. As the nuns sobbed into their robes one of the women in our group moved amongst them with tissues in a gesture of compassion. They were too sad to even acknowledge her kindness and just held the tissues to their streaming eyes. Without exception tears and sobs were coming from every nun and most of them were bent at the waist and shuddering with remembered experiences. We knew that if a nun was arrested for any reason she could never return to her nunnery. So many of their companions had simply disappeared and they had no way of knowing if they were dead or alive and perhaps suffering.

I was experiencing a unique moment in my life and every other tourist in the room felt the same privilege. I had a burning desire to take a photo and capture this moment for Newsweek so the world could share in the outpouring of grief. But along with others I did not raise my camera. Princess Diana had only just died and we were all acutely aware of intruding into a moment of such passion and sorrow. Somehow it would have seemed gauche and inappropriate. Besides, I doubt if any of us could have focused our cameras because of our own tears. Our actions were also tempered by the thought that if the picture was ever published and the nunnery identified then the nuns would face further torture.

It was incredible that when our group all discussed the incident later that we had all had the same misgivings about intruding into a sacred moment and the same fears of repercussions for the nuns if we had done so. There are times when I wish I had taken just one photo to send to His Holiness alone so he could envision the depth of despair in that room with all the maroon robed figures hunched over in grief and utter sadness. I guess that is a simplistic thought as I am sure he is already fully aware of the sorrows of his people and the commitment of the nuns of his country. Our silent gift to the nuns was expressed in our eyes. In our hearts we made our own decisions. This book is part of my pledge.

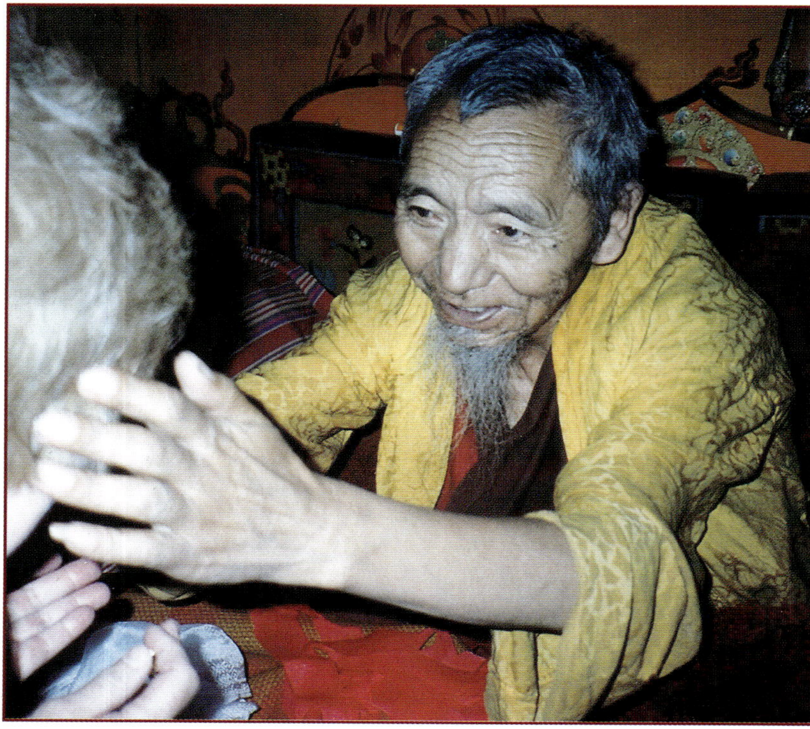

Chapter Six
MISINFORMATION

Those of us who live in the "free world" have very little concept of the propaganda machine which is the essence of modern China. Many of us have travelled in Moslem countries where the call to prayer echoes across the countryside in the early morning hours beckoning the faithful to praise Allah. If your beliefs do not compel you to rise you can snuggle under the blankets and be lulled back to sleep by the haunting melodies which linger in the air.

Modern Tibet, on the other hand, is hellish at dawn. In every town across the land the people rise to the sound of Chinese music blaring through loudspeakers. Some of the songs are harmonious to our ears but others jangle every fibre of your being. If you can cast your mind back to High School days, when messages crackled over the old PA systems into our classrooms from over zealous Principals, you will have an idea of the decibel level which blasts across the land. Maybe the volume has something to do with the fact that most of the occupying forces are really young soldiers who probably enjoy their music played loudly enough to deafen any sane adult.

It may seem a strange thing to say but I actually felt sorry for many of the Chinese soldiers who were posted in Tibet. The Tibetan plateau is a massive isolated area of splendid stark scenery. However, to young Chinamen from bustling cities it

would be tantamount to being sent to purgatory. The military are housed in stereotyped rectangular barracks which have no redeeming aesthetic qualities. The compounds are almost identical throughout the land. The boredom of the soldiers must be acute. No wonder so many of them are trigger happy.

If a military person manages to obtain a posting in Lhasa it means that he will be able to experience some city life, such as it is. The presence of the soldiers in the city is very evident and in some of the bars and cafes it feels as though you are in an old World War I or II movie where the troops in uniform mingle with the locals. There are parts of Lhasa where you can now find women plying their ancient trade outside neon lit shopfronts, but Lhasa is still a quiet backwater of a city.

Before the Chinese arrived Lhasa was only thought to have a population of around twenty-five thousand. Today there are one hundred and fifty thousand in the city but more than fifty percent are Chinese. Incredibly, there is now a "Tibetan

Quarter" in the Eastern part of Lhasa because so much of the city carries a Chinese influence.

It is believed the entire population of the Tibetan Autonomous Region is only around two and a half million but it is very difficult to obtain statistics which are known to include Chinese nationals, although they are now believed to outnumber Tibetans. If all Tibetans are counted throughout the Chinese regions, which include large portions of what we would have known as North-Eastern Tibet, their numbers could be as high as six million.

More than a million Tibetans are known to have died since the Chinese invasion. The scale of this devastation should be the cause of great shame amongst the Chinese perpetrators. When we see this statistic we become aware that nearly half of central Tibet's people died as victims of the Chinese 'liberation'.

I can imagine the Chinese defence of these statistics. I imagine them saying that of course this percentage of the population could have died over a fifty year time span. But our question must always be - at what ages did these people die and what was the cause of their deaths?

The communist Chinese use standardised methods of obtaining information from all Tibetans. These are the same methods deployed against any Chinese citizen if the Party wishes to obtain information. During the time of rule by the Gang of Four, which did not end until Mao's death in 1976, interrogations of any person, in any part of China, were particularly brutal. Therefore, in Tibet, where they were trying to erase Buddhism and create a new belief system of blind allegiance to the Party, there were horrific deeds of inhuman cruelty.

The people were interrogated constantly on their "sins" against the party but it was very difficult to know what constituted a "sin". You were not a good Party member unless you informed on your fellow man and this was particularly difficult for Tibetans.

The whole Party structure depended on "study sessions" in which groups of Tibetans were brought together and told of the "new way". These sessions rapidly deteriorated into times of accusation and intimidation.

The sessions were frequently followed by "thanzings" where Tibetans were made to beat their fellow women and men. Even the children were forced to assist. Many thousands died as a result of these public beatings and many more were left crippled and brain damaged. If someone refused to co-operate they were also beaten. It was an absolute no win situation for the Tibetans.

Although it was almost unheard of in their society prior to 1950, hundreds, and probably thousands, of Tibetans turned to suicide as the only means of escape from the horror of living under the communists. It is believed many chose this option, not so much because of their own suffering, but because of their despair at having to accuse and beat their friends and members of their own families.

Tibetans were constantly forced to deny the four "olds" which were their thoughts, custom, culture and habits. The biggest problem was that they were never sure just how they were to do this. One elderly Tibetan, Palden Gyatso, who was imprisoned in Tibet for thirty years, relates the story of a day when he simply flicked water off his hands. He was immediately accused of making an offering to a Buddhist deity and punished. He also recalls the time when he and his fellow monks were asked,

"Who nurtured you?"

He says they all gave the same answer,

"Our mothers."

They were wrong. The correct answer was that proletarian labour had nurtured them. They were trying to comprehend a new vocabulary and new concepts and at all times they were fearful of giving the wrong answer.

I really had no concept of the forcefulness, intensity and constancy of the Chinese propagandists until I read Palden Gyatso's book, "Fire Under the Snow" which he has written since he escaped Tibet in 1992. He now lives in exile in Dharamsala.

This humble man began his religious life as a naive intelligent young monk in a rural monastery. He then spent time at the famous Drepung Monastery in Lhasa. After his family recalled him to serve in his hometown monastery, the XIV Dalai Lama visited the town and said that Palden Gyatso should return to Drepung to continue his studies. The word of the Dalai Lama is gospel and Palden Gyatso was very content with his life back at Drepung.

Once the Dalai Lama went into exile in 1959 the problems with Chinese "study sessions" exacerbated and the repercussions were felt throughout Tibet. Along with thousands of fellow monks Palden Gyatso spent years being interrogated, abused, accused, shackled, strung up and beaten. His mouth was severely burnt when an electric prod was forced onto his tongue. As a result of this torture his teeth fell out. He nearly starved to death many times. Since his escape he has found that ultimately his life was only spared because of intervention from Amnesty International.

I cannot find the words to explain how deeply his story moved me. This is the reality of the fanatically meted out injustices of the Chinese radicals. His book also recounts the moving story of the daring and courage of many Tibetans who have already died, and of those who are still willing, to this day, to lay down their lives trying to help their fellow men. Read it and weep.

The Chinese stripped families of possessions and accused and abused according to your "class" at the time of the invasion. If you were perceived to have been from an affluent background you were subject to ever harsher and more constant "sessions" and punishments.

Even objects were defined as "remnants of the old feudal society" or "new socialist objects". This meant that books, many items of furniture, even traditional wooden bowls and anything coloured maroon or gold, all had to be burnt.

All the gentle aspects of Tibetan life were being annihilated and the only hope for the people to cling to, was that they knew His Holiness was safely in exile and would be trying to rally help for his people.

In this age of mass communication we can not plead ignorance. We know what these vicious invaders have done. We must speak out so loudly that our words are heard by the everyday citizens of China. It is only by raising awareness that we can help the Dalai Lama in his mission of peace.

His Holiness does not hate the Chinese. He is meticulous in ensuring there is a distinction between the ruthless, merciless communist zealots and the rest of the Chinese people. He reaches out gently and hopes for an understanding born from compassion. He longs for peace for all the world, not just for

Tibet. An address he gave in 1984 says it all:

"Irrespective of varying degrees of development and economic disparities, continents, nations, communities, families, in fact, all individuals are dependent on one another for their existence and well-being. Every human being wishes for happiness and does not want suffering. By clearly realising this, we must develop mutual compassion, love, and a fundamental sense of justice. In such an atmosphere there is hope that problems between nations and problems within families can be gradually overcome and that people can live in peace and harmony. Instead, if people adopt an attitude of selfishness, domination and jealousy, the world at large, as well as individuals will never enjoy peace and harmony. Therefore, I believe that human relations based on mutual compassion and love are fundamentally important to human happiness."

Tensin Gyatso, the XIV Dalai Lama of Tibet, seeks peace for all.

He is well informed, well travelled and not naive. He genuinely believes in the innate goodness of people and their potential to act with compassion. He knows that many people are not aware of what has happened in his country.

There are also millions in China who simply do not understand the true situation in Tibet because of misinformation. I have read translations of books about Tibet which are available in Chinese libraries. Their history books state that the imperialist British and Americans were constantly trying to overpower Tibet. Their authors state that the Chinese are the liberators of the Tibetan people.

I was saddened to realise that some of these inaccurate books have Tibetan authors. Although we do not hear much about them, there are Tibetans who have chosen the easier path of total co-operation with their Chinese oppressors.

We cannot blame the Chinese students for absorbing their history lessons and believing what is in their books. Rather, we must try to clarify the truth for them. Thankfully we live in an age where all cultures are becoming more aware of each other. We know that Chinese students hear about entertainers from the west as well as those from their powerful nation. Our thanks must go to famous campaigners such as Richard Gere who are willing to give so much time and energy to clarifying the Tibetan issue on a global scale.

Richard has been instrumental in establishing the "International Campaign for Tibet" and "Tibet House" in New York which aims to preserve Tibet's cultural heritage. He is a member of the "Committee of 100 for Tibet" which also includes John Cleese and ninety-eight other high profile supporters.

Chapter Seven
THE PEACEFUL PATH

The people of China and Tibet are folk like you and me. As babies we all start life with a pretty even playing field. Our prejudices and emphatic aggression in life only come after we have observed someone who has had the power to influence our thinking. We westerners find the Tibetans so refreshing with their gentle outlook but their attitude of caring for all life is attributable to the way in which they are guided as children by their elders and peers. Their role models show by their actions that all life is precious. Tibetan children learn to respect the earth itself and the creatures which move upon it. It is a simple matter of believing in something strongly enough and holding on to that belief as you go about your daily tasks.

There are millions of children on this planet who have never absorbed the wonders of nature nor even experienced the joy of owning a pet. We actively promote the eradication of every 'creepy crawley' bug which dares to occupy one square inch of what we regard as 'our space'. If we don't understand the place of a bug in the cycle of life we simply spray it or squash it dead. We are paranoid about evicting from our environment anything which does not please us. It is difficult to respect the miracle of the creation of a tiny insect when the only close up you ever see of one is as a smudge where you have erased its life.

This is not a message to convert the world to Buddhism. Buddhists are a most non-evangelical lot. They are quite happy for you to be whatever you wish. Probably one of the assets of the religion is this lack of fanaticism and non-judgement of each other. I am presenting this view to you as a simple fact which is evident in the Tibetan culture.

Even the spiritual leader of the Tibetans, the Dalai Lama himself, does not bother to preach at people. He speaks of what he sees and what he would like to see, but he does not ask all Buddhists to march around the world flashing his ideas to the masses.

I am sure many of you believe the Dalai Lama would have to be a vegetarian because of his position. Rather, His Holiness openly states in his autobiography that he tried being a vegetarian and found he did not feel healthy enough and now he includes meat in his diet.

Many Tibetans are like those of us who eat meat as long as we don't have to kill it ourselves. In Tibet there were always a few Moslem butchers for this purpose. There are many in the world who would be highly critical of this aspect of the Dalai Lama's life but it is of no consequence. It is a non-issue to a Buddhist. Your life choices are your own.

However, the simple truth appears to be, if your childhood develops around peace loving adults, you will almost certainly absorb this influence through a type of osmotic process. The splendour of nature and the nurturing power of animals are also beneficial. This webbed effect of the interrelation of environment and behaviour has been researched by many a more interested scholar than I.

My hope is that our technological world will encompass and make allowances for such simple facts. We live in an age when a rapidly expanding network of worldwide contacts is becoming the norm for every citizen. Let us hope that the internet will pave the way for glimmerings of world understanding as people everywhere link into communications which may blossom into friendships. Thankfully, most humans find that familiarity lowers a tendency towards aggression which may have been directed against a formerly unknown person.

Communication is probably the most powerful tool in our modern world and the Chinese leaders are fully aware of its power to sway their population.

One morning when we were in Gyantse, one of the larger

towns in Tibet, I decided to spend a morning relaxing in my hotel room. As I read my book I also turned on the television just to see what sort of programs were beamed in Tibet. I must confess to expecting to view shows quite beneath our western standards.

I had one of the biggest surprises of my life. My book was immediately tossed aside and I spent the next three hours flicking through the channels.

There were soap operas with the characters dressed to the nines, just as they are in the American productions but with Chinese actors. Their houses were also based on western decor and although I couldn't understand the language I could guess that the scripts were also similar.

Movies were on two other stations and one even had English subtitles. One of the films I saw was obviously from India where the standards of film making are excellent.

On a documentary program which was transmitted in English and subtitled in Chinese I even saw an interview with the Australian male tap dancing group known as "Tap Dogs". There were music programs and variety shows.

Every time there was a break between programs something amazing occurred. In addition to commercials there were incredible promotional spots. The most beautiful Chinese women I have ever seen, with full make up and designer clothes, would appear on screen in video clips which had been produced to the highest standards in the world. The women were invariably singing songs of national pride. They would be singing in Chinese but there were both Tibetan and English subtitles. I was astonished at some of the words to the songs. They ran along theses lines:

"From the East to the West
From the North to the South
Our homeland is beautiful
We are all united
We love our country
We are all together
We are proud to belong"

Backing the singers were scenes of development projects which faded into beautiful scenery. Images of majesty and futuristic fantasy drifted across the screen

Nothing, had prepared me for the realisation that China was drawing her people into the biggest web of nationalistic pride one could imagine. I had believed Americans were patriotic! The Chinese are making them look positively apathetic.

I am not criticising this propaganda machine. I am simply fascinated by its enormity and efficiency and unifying power. Every day the Chinese people are hearing the same message. We are united. We are great. We are proud to be Chinese.

The younger generation of Tibetans are hearing the same message. We must hope that their own culture does not disappear under this onslaught. As His Holiness himself said:

"We are becoming a minority in our own country. The new Chinese have created a Chinese apartheid which threatens to overwhelm and absorb us.......This is China's idea of a "final solution" to its Tibetan problem."

By the time my roomate came back from her morning tour I was agog with what I had seen.

"My God," I said to her. "Their message is so powerful they almost converted me to their Utopian vision and I've only watched it for one morning!"

China's population is listed as 1.2 billion and a fair percentage of its citizens are on the receiving end of a professionally marketed boost in national pride. Let us hope that someone in charge of the information which goes to air will also promote peace, rather than aggression, to such numbers of people.

Chapter Eight

LHASA TODAY

Lhasa itself, in 1950, would have been amongst the most beautiful cities on this planet. Some of the sites in and around Lhasa are still breathtaking in their splendour and make you yearn for the days when they were in their prime.

A magical tributary of the Brahmaputra River named the Kyi Chu, flows swiftly through the town. It sparkles with golden daytime stars created by the sunlight catching on its ruffled surface. It is a clear snow fed waterway but city life is destroying its charm. Once there was a tree covered island captured in the river. Now there is an island bare of trees and covered with bars and offices.

The Chinese leaders are encouraging their citizens to treat Tibet like the old Wild West. They want young men to come here to their 'frontier town' and try to make their fortunes and establish Lhasa as a Chinese city. They are rapidly succeeding and now there are more Chinese than Tibetans in the country. Their aim is to have 60 million Chinese immigrants in Tibet by 2020.

Those of you who travelled to Singapore around thirty years ago will be able to picture the type of development occurring in Lhasa today. The main streets are lined with strip shopping with the typical Asian shops which roll down their metal doors at night. Most buildings are still only two stories high, but new hotels are springing up and companies such as Telecom are starting to build modern office blocks. Unusual sights like the modern sports stadium seem incongruous in this predominantly low-rise setting.

On the outskirts of Lhasa suburbs are springing up with project housing developments not unlike those in the west. Row upon row of two storey dwellings are lined up side by side, generally with the design changing approximately every six houses. These homes, with front and back garden areas, are for the more affluent and some Tibetans manage to purchase them with money which is sent to them from family members who are living in exile. Inside the homes the layout is familiar with kitchens and lounge rooms downstairs and bedrooms upstairs.

One difference is that the braver of the Tibetan families will always turn a spare room or corner into a quiet place for meditation and worship. These rooms often hold an altar with Buddhist pictures on show, but photos of the Dalai Lama are always kept in secret places in case the authorities visit. This supposed freedom to follow Buddhism can change at any time. The last purge of Buddhist material was as recent as 1992 when house to house searches were carried out. In 1995 a ban was again placed on any items related to the Dalai Lama, including tapes, pictures, prayers, books or speeches. Modern Tibetans live in a constant 'police state' where they almost have to ask permission to breathe. They are not free to travel and can be arrested without trial for trivial offences. Speaking to a foreigner can be perceived as a 'crime'. Singing Tibetan songs or gathering without a permit are liable to lead to jail terms.

Tibetan furnishings are quite colourful and settees, which are more like long divans, are generally covered in gaily coloured woven rugs and heaped with cushions. Hospitality is legendary and sometimes you simply cannot believe how many cups of tea you have consumed, or how many glasses of chang, the local barley beer. Tourists generally love both these brews, or cannot swallow either. I simply told myself they were both made with natural produce and therefore had to be good for me and drank everything in sight. I could have become quite addicted to chang. It has a similar bite to the South American Pisco Sour.

It is still common for several generations of a family to live under the same roof. Life in these homes appears to run in a very similar routine to our western homes a couple of decades ago. Grandma is usually around to mind the small children as the young women are now liable to work in office jobs or in hotels in the same types of jobs as their husbands. Suburban families often have a pet dog with its kennel at the front door. It would be lovely to close this paragraph with "….. and God's in his Heaven, all's right with the world." However, we know that for the Tibetan people this life is simply an existence until the Dalai Lama can return and they can live their lives without fear.

The slabs of concrete which are stacked together to create

boxlike apartments overshadow the cute original Tibetan homes. Tibetan architecture created pretty chocolate box images. Timber framed windows with flowerboxes. Whitewashed walls highlighted with brightly painted doorways. The ever present pleated valances which ripple in the breeze over doorways and windows and along the eaves. These scenes are being eclipsed by the jarring sight of the incongruous grey high rise developments.

Lhasa Today

All roads in the centre of Lhasa are surfaced and crumbling footpaths line the main streets. In common with most Chinese cities concrete rules supreme and creates an ugliness when left in its basic drab grey. The city area is totally flat and really easy for cyclists. Traffic is still manageable with tourist coaches and trucks and taxis and cyclists all mingling in that inimitable way which seems to only gel in countries where pedestrians and livestock believe they are just as important as vehicles. It is not uncommon for a flock of sheep or goats to be herded down the main street. Taxis, in the main, appear a bit battered but the drivers are very friendly and it is the same fare wherever you go in the city so there are no disputes.

Chapter Nine
HOMES OF A HUMBLE MAN

Prior to the Chinese invasion the citizens of Lhasa lived in harmony with nature and their surroundings. Early travellers commented on the exquisite flowers which graced every available nook and cranny. Tibetan craftsmanship was extremely advanced and their architecture is amazing. For a very long time the Potala Palace was the largest skyscraper in the world. This massive structure of well over 1,000 rooms is so well designed that it even sits on a copper base to enable it to withstand earthquake movements.

In the midst of the city landscape the Potala Palace rises in solitary splendour on a craggy hilltop. It has often been referred

to as one of the wonders of this world and deserves every accolade. It is an awesome building. It actually knocks the breath out of you it is such a splendid sight.

The front of the Palace faces an immense courtyard area which is now a field of concrete used for gatherings. When you stand on this paved area and look back up at the Potala it takes a minute to realise what is jarring your senses. Then the penny drops - flying dead centre on the rooftop is the red flag of the Chinese Republic. It is a rare sight to even see a Tibetan flag anymore, let alone seeing one flying in Tibet.

How I wished I had been a visitor to the Potala when the monks still called it home. The Chinese have turned the Potala into a museum. Admittedly it is a Tibetan Museum but wonderful artwork and statues and doorways with enormous brass handles and decorated stairwells, massive assembly halls and rooftop gardens are simply not the same without the monks in their maroon and gold robes.

There are no robed monks living in the Potala any more. The few monks tending the butter lamps wear western dust jackets in drab greens and greys and even then you cannot be sure if they are genuine monks or imposters. There is no chanting resonating through the immensely thick walls and vibrating into your soul. The sounds and smells which once would have pervaded this palace have been replaced by a thinness. The texture and richness of the Potala is silenced.

Remember the hush that fell on the world when Princess Diana died. That same hush is in the Potala.

For all its magnificence the Potala is definitely an overpowering building and the young Dalai Lama actually preferred to spend as much time as possible at the Norbulingka, his Summer Palace. The Norbulingka is only four miles from the Potala but

Homes Of A Humble Man

it is like entering another world. While the Potala commands imposing views of Lhasa in all directions the Summer Palace is laid out in a beautiful garden setting on flat terrain. The Summer Palace is completely surrounded by trees and gardens and offered the young ruler a freedom which could not exist in the Potala. Here was a setting where pets could abound and a zoo was even set up in the grounds.

One Stone for Tibet

From his rooms the Dalai Lama could lift his eyes to the mountains that ringed Lhasa but still have some privacy. In 1959 he was to escape across the very mountains he saw from his bedroom each morning. They are barren formidable mountains and this was a harsh route to travel but it was the way chosen for him by the Nechung Oracle.

Normally travellers would enter and leave Lhasa by passing through the beautiful Yarlung Valley which lines the banks of the Brahmaputra River. That is a vista for kings to behold but the road to freedom is often a much harder road to travel.

Sadly, the gardens of the Norbulingka are now neglected but the majestic trees grace the pathways with dappled shadows. It is a spiritual experience to walk under the huge coloured archway at the entrance and know you are now in this restful

haven. As you wander along the wide walkways you can glimpse alluring areas which are closed to the public. Inaccessible faded archways beckon. A gazebo in the distance appears to be covered in a profusion of weeds The outer buildings for the Palace wear a tired facade but their architecture blends them into the garden setting and faded paintwork traces memories of bygone days.

Tourists are permitted to enter the Summer Palace which greets you with a vivid entrance in myriad jewel colours. We were allowed to wander through the private apartments of His Holiness and feel the essence of his home.

The Summer Palace is not grand but it exudes an atmosphere of peacefulness. It is a two storey dwelling with apartments for His Holiness, reception rooms, and a suite of rooms for his family. It had so obviously been a happy dwelling because of its setting and the profusion of colour throughout the rooms. All that was missing were the serene and happy faces of Tibetans who would have loved to work in this Palace of beauty.

Instead, we were accompanied on our tour by several of the ever present 'men in grey'. These Chinese gentlemen are never a part of your tour group but just 'happen' to be touring at the same time as you.

We had a real giggle at Samye Monastery when three of us closely examined a wall panel of painted buddhas. As we looked we could see that each figure was minutely different from the next. Obviously the artist had taken delight in his skill at making all the images appear the same from a few feet away. After we moved on, our 'men in grey' stood in front of the images for several minutes with puzzled looks on their faces. I don't think they ever found our 'secret' and to this day they probably wonder what we were up to.

It is now a fact of life that tourist sites attract gift shops and there are several just inside and outside the Norbulingka entrance. The larger of these, along with the hotel gift shops, now include many Chinese articles amongst their Tibetan wares. Already it is obvious that Lhasa is becoming a suburban outpost of Beijing.

Chapter Ten
THE POTALA

It was only a few weeks before I left for Tibet that I finally saw a perspective of the Potala which was new to me. An artist had drawn the westerly aspect and you could see just how the Palace was perched on a lone hilltop. This opened a new sense of wonder for me because all previous photos I had seen were taken from directly in front of the building. I could not wait to see the back of the Potala.

I was not disappointed. This magnificent building is grand from every aspect. You can completely circle the Potala and view it from every angle. Leafy gardens sprinkle the hillside behind the Palace even though suburbia now encroaches on its grounds. I

Front View

had never given much thought to the day to day workings of a building of this scale so I was soon to discover another practical aspect of the layout. As you approach the Potala from the front you can veer to the left and drive up a winding roadway which only the most adventurous coach drivers tackle because of the sheer drop on one side. However, if you are fortunate enough to be travelling with one of these daredevils it means you save yourself an exhausting climb to reach the entrance for tourists.

After being in Lhasa for a few days you become aware of the great number of tourists who become severely debilitated from the effects of high altitude. These effects are exacerbated by activity and many tourists have to be flown out of Lhasa to avoid death from embolisms. Generally your body adapts to the altitude after a few days but when we were crossing the Tibetan Plateau we came across travellers who were on a cycling holiday. They were really testing their bodies by cycling over mountain passes at altitudes of up to 18,000 feet with icy winds blowing and clouds of dust thrown up by cattle trucks and coaches along the route.

We stopped at an isolated town for a noodle lunch and around an hour later one of these cyclists was brought in in the back of a four wheel drive vehicle which had been flagged down by his group. He was wrapped in a thermal sleeping bag and completely still. Four of his friends lifted him from the vehicle as though he was a corpse. He was carried into the only inn in the town. In our language this establishment would have been fortunate to rate even one star but it was a haven in a stark landscape. This is a story with no ending because we moved on but it brought home to all of us just how quickly the mountains can highlight our human frailty. Even climbing the extra few hundred feet from the base to the top of the Potala can exhaust some people.

The Potala

To enter the Potala from the coach bay on the western side there is a short walk up an incline and through one of the majestic Tibetan gateways. Tibetan gates and doorways generally have carved portals decorated in brilliant colours which frame massive wooden doors with simply enormous round brass handles. These handles are generally many times the size of a ring you would see through a bull's nose and may be draped with exquisite fabrics. A charming coffee table book could be produced featuring only the doors of Tibet.

We were entering the Potala through part of the 'red' walled section. When you view the Potala it has only two colours to the facade - either a stark white or an unusual reddish brown colour. Even centuries after it has been built it is still not wise to lean against the walls as the colours come off on your clothes. What a souvenir!

We joined a queue to enter the Palace and as we waited I looked up into the sky. There were fourteen buzzards circling right above us. They appeared to be in total harmony and every now and then they would break their formation and when they did so I was fascinated by their behaviour. They consistently broke away in pairs, never alone.

Finally we were inside the Potala and my first impression was of its immense size. The corridors are wide enough for several men to walk side by side and the ceilings seemed to average more than twenty feet high and in some places soared several stories high. It felt like entering an Aladdin's cave because almost immediately we turned on our torches. We were led past some tombs of earlier Dalai Lamas and incredible statues of Buddhist deities which were draped with offerings of scarves and gifts of money. These offerings are rarely removed and build up on the statues and gradually become covered with a film of soot from

the ever present butter lamps which are tended in front of every statue.

The scarves which are offered to the gods are the same special scarves called khatas which Tibetans offer as a sign of greeting or reverence. This tradition is similar in vein to the offering of a lei in Hawaii. When visiting a Tibetan in his home or even at a restaurant or in a monastery it is not uncommon to exchange white scarves. It is one of the joys of travelling in Tibet to come home at the end of a long day with several flowing khatas around the necks of both men and women. The scarves are long, flimsy and drape easily and can be bought in differing qualities. In the Barkhor, the central market of Tibet, you can buy them for as little as twenty cents each. However, they are also available with splendid patterns woven in the finest silk.

We were also delighted to be allowed to share in another quaint Tibetan custom. As a term of endearment or respect the Tibetans may choose to put "la" at the end of your name. It is similar to the use of "San" in Japan or "tu" in France. Our Tibetan guides used "la" freely when addressing each other and laughed heartily when we joined in the practice. By the end of our tour we could not use each others Christian names without tacking on a "la".

One of our group said he had read that the title of the mythical land of Shangri-la was borne in this delightful way.

We were not quite ready to call ourselves Tibetologists but we were feeling quite chuffed with some of the things we had learnt.

We found the local pronunciation of Potala quite simple to master. The Tibetans say "Po" as in yoyo. In the middle is a quick "t". Not tee, simply "t" for train. Then, if you can cast yourself over to the Middle East, the easiest way to remember the last part of the word is to think of dear old "Allah" as in Allah be praised. When you run it all together you get Po-t-ala. The emphasis is on the "Po". The rest simply flows behind.

The Potala has a magical attraction to people who love mazes and meandering pathways. There are bends and twists and nooks and crannies which then open into simply enormous galleries and chanting halls where some statues are two stories tall. Pilgrims seem to know where they are headed and at times there are 'traffic jams' of people outside a tiny room of particular significance to the Buddhists. Jaded tourists are often heard murmuring "seen one monastery seen them all" just as many travellers do when they are touring the churches of Europe.

For me, though, it was all so different that I could have explored for days. I was particularly interested in a game we were playing amongst ourselves of trying to pick the 'genuine' monks from the imposters. Although the Potala is now a museum there are a token number of men in attendance, all of whom are dressed in the same bland dustjackets. We were told these men are mostly monks and that is why we were using our 'psychic' powers to distinguish who was who. We liked to think we could feel the 'essence' of the true followers of the Buddhist pathway but we had no way of testing our theories.

To set the atmosphere for the tourists, the yak butter lamps in front of many statues are constantly tended as they would have been when the Potala was a monastery. Huge brass, copper and bronze cauldrons and smaller silver and gold chalices are filled almost to the brim with butter which liquefies with the heat from the burning wicks glowing on its surface. The golden glow from butter lamps creates a mystical atmosphere and the mingled smell of slightly rancid butter and candlewick pervades everything.

Of course the 'monks' have another use as well. They are there to collect the money which is required to be paid before a tourist is allowed the privilege of taking a photo. All over Tibet monks have their tin cash boxes which contain the bounty to be handed to the Chinese. In Shigatse it cost forty US dollars to take a photo of the

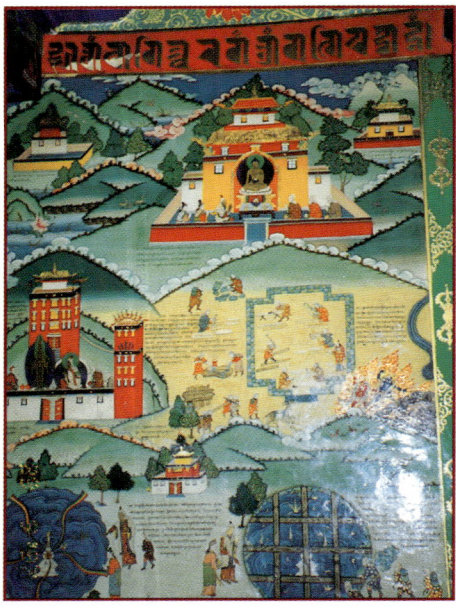

80 foot high Maitreya Buddha, the Buddha of the future, which is said to be coated with three hundred pounds of gold. One could almost believe the Chinese have taken lessons in extortion from some of the more avaricious Egyptian tourist guides.

Some of the grand halls in the Potala have upper levels with balconies which look down onto the ceremonial areas and everywhere there is colour. Embroidered silk banners still decorate the walls. Patchwork brocade pieces quilted into exquisite designs and enhanced with tiny gold bells are wrapped around massive columns or hang from the ceilings as frames for the beauty of the surroundings. In the higher halls sunlight beams through windows which are more like skylights positioned way up high where the walls meet the ceilings and the whole scene changes as the sunbeams move through the rooms. Grand columns are a feature of the architecture of many Tibetan halls and if they are not painted maroon they are often carved and highly decorated and point the way to magnificent ceiling panels.

Buddhism is a religion which encourages ceremony and praise and there is a joy in viewing the statues. One of the more amazing sights was the group of statues with bright blue hair or headdresses which make them look exactly like Madge from the cartoon series "The Simpsons".

Students of Buddhism gasp in amazement at the sheer immensity of statues which they have only seen represented in smaller copies. The source of much wonderment for most of us was the size of the jewels which are inlaid in the statues. Huge

pieces of turquoise and jade are exquisite against the gold and brass. I have heard that the Chinese have a habit of closing off certain statues to the public while 'restoration' takes place. It is believed that during these times the precious stones are replaced with imitations.

There are still examples of unbelievable Tibetan craftsmanship retained in special showrooms. Some displays depict whole

miniature palaces and cities. No one could accuse the Tibetans of lacking skills with fine metals and jewels and the world knows of the expertise of dedicated monks who create the finest sand mandalas.

An interesting conversion in the Potala is the 'tea house' which is set up in a type of glass and timber framed pergola. There, travellers from around the world can take a break and lounge on typical Tibetan carpeted divans while they sip their tea and exchange tales of their journeys.

After hours spent exploring we began to move down, which was a much better idea than attempting to move up. Even in the Potala many of the Tibetan steps are made of timber and brass with very steep rails and need to be negotiated with the same care as ships ladders.

We stepped down one of the unique Tibetan staircases which are railed off into three sections. Anyone may use the left or the

The Potala

right sections to go up or down, but the centre of the staircase is reserved for His Holiness alone. Throughout Tibet you will see the centre sections of the staircases cordoned off with ropes and with offerings sometimes placed on the steps to ensure no commoner ever tries to set foot on this sacred space.

Once we reached the bottom of the stairs we were in dazzling sunlight and as we looked around we realised we were in a large asphalt courtyard which was open to the sky. We were actually on a part of the roof of the Potala. Each of us had dreamt of this moment and now it was a reality.

Then some real fun began. Once again we stepped down into immense corridors which were painted with bright patterns arranged as friezes at the top and bottom of the walls. As we moved along we came to stone staircases within the roofed corridors. We descended on immensely broad cobbled steps with smoothly worn edges similar to those found outdoors in many European cities. And then came a wondrous discovery which I will never forget!

As we emerged into bright sunshine we were standing on a landing. We peered over the balustrade and beneath us we could see the rooftops of the buildings which are in front of the Potala. To get to the bottom we were to walk down the most wondrous stairway in the world. It had never occurred to me that the zig zag white wall in front of the Palace was hiding stairs made of ancient slabs of stone. I closed my eyes and visualised the slow progression of thousands of monks as they moved out of the building and down to the ceremonial courtyard in front of the Palace.

The steps were wide and shallow and many men could have walked down them shoulder to shoulder. We slowly descended, taking photos as we reached each landing. Beautiful pink and white daisy-like flowers called Cosmos grew like weeds out of every available crevice. The feathery foliage whispered against the bright white walls. This was a scene from bygone days. I loved the scale of the Potala. Everything was larger than life.

As we came down to earth we had to negotiate the predictable "T" shirt alley to get back to our coach. But even then we had another thrill. A lady was standing in front of our coach with a huge black yak. For the first time we had a chance to stroke one of these mighty beasts as he stood as placidly as any house pet. His proud head was adorned with red tassels, braids and beads. His role in life was to be the 'male model' in dozens of photo shoots daily. He came at a price, but he was darn good looking!

A male yak looks similar to a bison in stature but he is very broad across the back and flanks and he sports a very thick long coat which almost drags on the ground. It would take around six horses tails bound together to match one yak tail. They really are handsome animals.

Yaks are completely acclimatised in Tibet and do not fare at all well if they are taken out of their mountain environment. On the hillsides they are as nimble-footed as goats. One day we watched as a herd ran down a near vertical gradient, towards a riverbed. We all held as our breath as we waited for these mighty beasts to slip and roll on the loose shale on the hillside, but it never happened.

We watched the males as they grouped together on either side of a shallow river and even in the river bed. Some of them rolled in the water and then stood up and shook their massive hairy coats like huge dogs. The funny thing was they were almost the size of baby elephants. Some lolled around in the sunshine and grazed when they felt so inclined. Others decided to charge at each other and engage in a bit of serious ground pawing, pushing and boisterous head-butting. In general though, they were a bit half hearted about their aggression and

after a few good shoves they ambled off and either sulked or feigned indifference by going for a dip instead.

Generally speaking yaks are black, but there are some beautiful variations in their coats ranging from creams to reds. The colours are very similar to those found in herds of alpacas.

On the day we stopped to watch the antics of the male yaks we came across the females and babies much higher up the valley. This was a bucolic scene with all the animals grazing peacefully and the chubby little yaks looking like stuffed toys dotted on the sparse landscape.

Chapter Eleven
THE BARKHOR

Most famous cities have a market place of distinction and in Lhasa there is the famous Barkhor. I found this a comparatively restful market where the traders did not push their wares under your nose. In one of the tiny shops which frame the rim of the market place we were enchanted by the intricate hairstyle of the proprietor. She was obviously from the Eastern area of Khan because her long black hair was woven with huge chunks of natural turquoise. While we were in her shop a handsome

warrior like man came to speak to us. Despite his size he had a gentle energy and soon had us roaring with laughter as he negotiated a "trade-off". He desperately wanted my Australian Akubra hat. It was a grand brimmed hat, the sort our Australian stockmen wear under our blazing skies. So, if you ever come across a tall, good looking dude in the Barkhor wearing an Aussie Akubra give him my regards. Meanwhile, I am the proud owner of a beautiful polished Tibetan gemstone. It is black on the almost round outer rim and fades through shades of grey to a white "eye" in the centre. The lady from the shop, whom I suspect was married to the handsome gentleman, 'assured' me we had negotiated a fair deal!

To me it was a pleasure to shop here and I loved the evident camaraderie amongst the stall owners. When we were buying prayer flags there was much joking about which size we would need.

Prayer flags are one of the traditions which seem to have persisted despite the new regime. Then again, there was a time when they were banned and maybe they are only available again in a bid to lull tourists into thinking all is well.

They are easy to tuck away in a travellers pack and I can imagine the satisfaction which a Tibetan must feel when he strings out his offerings in many isolated places and no-one is any the wiser as to who the culprit was. In a similar vein, the mantra of Om Mane Padme Hum is often marked out in stones in Tibetan lettering in the most out of the way places. Often, under cover of darkness, the locals rearrange stones which had spelt out Chinese propaganda, and create their own message of hope.

Prayer flags grace every peak in Tibet. There are times when you may feel you are standing on the most isolated spot on this

planet but when you look to the highest point there will be the inevitable strings of flags strung out between makeshift timber frames which are supported by rock cairns. The flags are also flown in the towns and around homes, anywhere the wind can pass by to whisper the prayers to the gods.

These flags start their life in brilliant colours which represent the natural elements. Red for fire, yellow for earth, blue for sky, white for clouds and green for water. With time they fade to a pale aqua, a pinky red and a bleached white and if you did not know otherwise you would swear the original colours were red, white and blue.

In her travels, Sorrel Wilby was told of deeper interpretations of the five colours of the flags.

She found they also reflect the Buddhist states of mind – form, feeling, recognition, karmic formation and consciousness.

At a higher level the colours stand for the five Buddhist wisdoms – the abilities to reflect what the mind sees; to compare; to differentiate; to accomplish and the perception of truth – Buddha-hood.

The colours of the flags can also be bought in the khatas. These wonderful scarves glow with the brilliant colours we see in the best silk.

The Barkhor is a special market because you must only walk around it in a clockwise direction. It is too bad if you feel the need to backtrack for a second look at something because you

are meant to go right around again. It is a great laugh to see the furtive faces of some tourists as they try to beat the system by walking backwards or sneaking around corners. There is a reason for this tradition because the Barkhor is right in front of the most revered temple in Tibet, the Jokhang and in this temple you definitely only move clockwise.

The Jokhang is situated on flat ground, so it does not stand out. The site, built over an ancient lake, was evidently chosen by a wife of the Tibetan King in the 600's. From that time the temple has housed the most revered statue in Tibet, the Sakyamuni Buddha. This statue, the most precious object in Tibet, was brought here at the time the Tibetans converted to Buddhism and has not been moved for 1300 years.

The Jokhang is the spiritual centre of all Tibet and houses many statues, shrines and murals. It is a sturdy old building which basically presents a facade of black, white and gold. It does not have the flamboyant colour schemes of rich reds, blues and brilliant emerald greens which grace some of the newer temples.

To enter the Jokhang you pass dozens of pilgrims prostrating themselves in the forecourt. From a standing position both men and women kneel, then lean forward in a sweeping motion and lie face down on the ground. After a couple of seconds they pull back into a kneeling pose and then stand upright again. This arduous

routine is repeated over and over while the smoke from two enormous kiln-like incense burners hovers in the air around them. It is awesome to see the glow on the faces of these people, some of whom have travelled great distances for this moment. Many of them have only reached the Jokhang by prostrating themselves along the entire route of their journey to this holy place.

As you step into a concrete courtyard you are surrounded by rows and rows of thousands of tiny butter lamps which are lit as offerings. Even in the daylight you feel the impact of the flickering lights.

We then turned left and wandered down avenues of brass prayer wheels, some of which were still spinning from the hands of the pilgrims in front of us. We too were welcome to turn the wheels of prayer, so long as we again did it in a clockwise direction! These drum shaped wheels which were around three feet tall were positioned at waist height so you felt you wanted to spin each one as you passed by. We completed one circumambulation of the covered walkway around the Jokhang and then entered the Temple.

There was a continuous line of pilgrims following the route through the Temple and in and out of the many Chapels within. We felt a certain amount of guilt because our guide bustled us past the patiently waiting locals. However, there was no animosity on their faces at all, only knowing smiles as we had

One Stone for Tibet

to rush through a place where they were happy to linger all day.

Our guide lead us into a quiet room where he told us the meaning of the well known Tibetan mantra of Om Mane Padme Hum - praise to the jewel in the heart of the lotus. One of the Monks overheard our stumbling attempts to repeat the chant and quietly joined in as a second coach. He then presented us all with our first khatas from a Temple and we felt exceedingly blessed by his gesture.

In the early years of the Cultural Revolution the Chinese annexed the monks' quarters at the Johkang and even renamed them Guesthouse No. 5. However, the monks were allowed back in 1980 and now live and train there and wear their traditional robes. Many of their long departed friends who have reincarnated as dogs doze in and around the Temple.

We were privileged to be guided by our friendly monk up onto the roof of the Temple. From here we had a stunning view of

the Potala and when we looked over the edge of the roof we were gazing down on the prostrating pilgrims and the Barkhor markets.

We were also overlooking the Police Station which was the centre of rioting when the Tibetans faced their own version of the Tienamen Square massacre in 1989. In March 1989 martial law was declared in Lhasa. In the wake of this declaration hundreds were killed and many thousands more were arrested. Accounts of this bloody massacre reached the west from tourists who were in the Barkhor at the time. They produced dramatic photos of monks with their clothing on fire and equally horrible sights. However, it was not until the Tienamen Square massacre later that year that world leaders fully realised the severity of what had occurred in Lhasa. It was difficult for people to grasp the fact that such vicious attacks were still being perpetrated.

Almost ten years later, as we gazed out over the Barkhor, we could see the surveillance cameras which were mounted on the Police Station roof, sweeping the crowds. The communist Chinese are ever vigilant.

Chapter Twelve
TASHI TSERING

On another corner of the Barkhor we climbed a staircase to meet a unique Tibetan. One of our group sought out the author of the book "The Struggle for Modern Tibet" and invited us along to meet him. Tashi Tsering is a genial man who was delighted to host our visit and plied us with numerous cups of tea and samples of the "best chang" in Tibet.

Tashi wrote his autobiography in an attempt to explain why he had chosen to return from exile and live in Lhasa.

Tashi was not born into the upper classes of the Tibetan feudal system and yet, even as a boy, he had a desire to better himself. He was chosen as a dancer in the Dalai Lama's Troupe and through this avenue received a sound education. Unfortunately, he also received some pretty brutal treatment from some of the senior monks and officials in Lhasa. This helped to convince him that changes needed to be made at the top and that people should be appointed to positions of power through their aptitude rather than their birthright. This is a fairly common concept on student campuses throughout the world.

Tashi was probably less patient that the average Tibetan. He firmly believed the ruling classes needed a bit of a shake up. He wasn't as patient as those who were waiting for the Fourteenth Dalai Lama to implement changes which were begun by the Thirteenth Dalai Lama.

Tashi was studying in India when the Dalai Lama escaped into exile. For a while he helped with the logistics of the Tibetan refugees in India but in 1960 he was offered a chance to study in America. His time in America was an immense learning curve for Tashi but he still believed that the Chinese were bringing new hope into Tibet with their proposed schools and hospitals.

Finally, despite warnings from his fellow Tibetans in exile, Tashi decided he wanted to go back to Lhasa to try to make a go of living under the supposedly progressive Chinese regime. He idealistically hoped that the communists may have been working towards a new society in Tibet where all men had an equal say. He knew he had the option of remaining in his comfort zone in America, but his heart told him to return to the country he loved and where he hoped to help create a new world.

It is easy for those of us in the west to be wise in hindsight. We are fully aware that egalitarianism is not a by product of totalitarian regimes. In fact, the regimes create rampant elitism because control is evinced through threat and fear.

In 1964 Tashi returned to Tibet and soon found he was way out of his depth. The Chinese did not care one whit for his opinions or good intent and in 1967 Tashi was denounced as a counterrevolutionary and sent into China as a prisoner. He spent six years doing enforced labour and had plenty of time to think about his life and the choices he had made. He had always felt that it was necessary to break down his country's theocratic ruling elite but the task was no longer his. The Chinese fulfilled that mission with total confidence that they were justified in their actions.

Tashi could never have envisaged the brutal manner in which this feat was accomplished. The Chinese not only effectively destroyed the system of Tibetan hierarchy but with it they had erased most of the tradition and culture from one of the most mature civilisations on this planet. They well and truly threw out the baby with the bathwater. They threw out the bath as well. They wanted the Tibetans purged and they managed to annihilate half of them and scare the daylights out of the rest.

The Chinese invaders have consistently tortured the Tibetans, but at certain times over the past 48 years they have made superficial attempts to moderate their actions.

In one of these ploys Tashi was allowed to become a Professor of English in Lhasa. Using his initiative he then set up 'night schools' because he could see that the Tibetan language was

disappearing through lack of use. Nowadays, he has established himself as a true academic after creating a Tibetan/Chinese/English Dictionary.

Tashi has an easy truce with the authorities. He has no children of his own and he ploughs all his own money and energy into building village schools where Tibetan is taught. In a quirky way he has achieved one of his goals, which was to bring education to the Tibetan village children. Just exactly what they are learning to write in Tibetan may be a moot point.

If there was freedom of speech in Tibet I could have asked him where the cut off price would have come if the scene was played again.

Chapter Thirteen
NUCLEAR CATACLYSM

Many of us became intensely interested in Tibet after first reading "The Third Eye" by T. Lobsang Rampa and then his many other books. According to Heinrich Harrer, Lobsang Rampa was an Englishman who had never been to Tibet and who quickly made his way to Canada when true Tibetologists tried to make his acquaintance. Although his information was evidently a created blend of Tibetan and other Asian cultures the simple fact is that he sold millions of books and whetted many appetites for Tibet. He facilitated a path for Europeans to imagine the mysteries of this land which was tucked away from the modern world.

Lobsang Rampa went into great detail about the herbal medicines of Tibet and the Chagpo Ri traditional hospital which was housed on the only other rocky outcrop in Lhasa. Sadly the Chinese destroyed this ancient hospital and built a radio tower on the peak.

A replacement hospital is now located in downtown Lhasa but it is a terrible shame it is no longer possible to see the original. However, there are several fascinating areas to explore where many of the original hospital books and samples are retained. There is a whole room of glass topped cabinets where you can peer at neatly labelled samples of herbs and mineral elements.

Then there is a room which I found magical. In Tibetan medicine there are approximately eighty thankhas which are

wall hangings with meticulous drawings of anatomy and other medical subjects. In this room the walls are lined with these magnificently produced poster sized charts, all of them with embroidered silk borders. I took dozens of close-up photos of these works of art, only to find that for only eighty US dollars you can now purchase a full colour book of the entire set. It is a huge, handsomely bound book and will remain one of my treasures forever. Thank heaven someone seems to have a little foresight about preserving some of these precious elements of history.

Herbal medicines are still a major part of the Tibetan culture. Even in the private clinics where doctors may also have traditional training as we know it, many herbal remedies are prescribed. It is fascinating to watch the doctors working hand in hand with their pharmacists who make up individual packages of herbs in the same way our chemists make up our prescriptions.

The herbs are collected from the Tibetan countryside and are now getting harder to obtain as development affects the patterns of growth in the countryside. Pollution is certain to affect some species and unfortunately it is now becoming a problem in Lhasa.

I will never forget my first view of this long awaited city of legends. There was a terrible haze over Lhasa which came from the cement works which are located on the outskirts of town, just beyond the Drepung Monastery. When the wind blows up the valley the fine grey dust simply blows over the city and

settles where it falls. Town Planning does not seem to be a priority for Chinese development projects.

Tibet was probably the first country on this planet to legislate on caring for the environment and wildlife. In 1642 the Fifth Dalai Lama decreed that animals and the environment must be protected. This law stood until the Chinese invasion.

Tibetans also guarded their natural resources and never dealt harshly with their lands. Since the Chinese occupation entire forests have been systematically destroyed in the beautiful eastern regions of Tibet. The resulting erosion from the destruction of an estimated seventy percent of the trees is causing dramatic changes in climate and living standards. The Chinese have not developed the skills to replant forests in this harsh climate and have simply let the cleared areas turn into deserts.

Many of the rare animal species which thrived in Tibet have been wiped out in the last half of this century because of the Chinese intervention. The 'blue sheep' are almost eradicated along with the unique 'white-lipped' deer. Snow leopards have passed into legend. There are hardly any wild yak or donkeys left roaming freely over the mountains and the flocks of geese and ducks no longer grace the skies.

Coupled with these horrific changes to the surface of the earth, the Chinese have also been mining in Tibet. Tibet's mountainsides contain untold mineral wealth in the form of plutonium, gold, copper, iron, lead, coal, oil and shale. The Chinese tend to strip mine but we did see evidence of massive tunnels going into mountainsides. The biggest problem is the lack of environmental care in these projects. World Health Authorities believe that chemical pollution and dust are having dramatic effects on the mine workers and those in the nearby communities. Many birth defects and deformities are being reported.

We even passed a 'secret' hospital where workers affected by uranium were tucked away from the world. This is entirely feasible as there are many stories circulating about the Chinese dumping nuclear waste in Tibet.

As I mentioned earlier, the Asian region is under dire ecological threat because of the cavalier attitude of the Chinese towards environmental issues. If the rivers become polluted at the 'top of the world' the South-East Asian region will be devastated. Now is the time for the rest of the world to act and insist on a Chinese evacuation of Tibet. Unless the "guardians" of this unique country are allowed home to try to rebalance the forces of nature and avert a nuclear disaster, we may be taught a terrible lesson.

We may all waken one day to find a cataclysm in Tibet will be the precursor of an immense tragedy in South-East Asia.

"There are none so blind, as those who will not see"

and

"none so weak as those who will not stand to be counted".

Chapter Fourteen
FAREWELL YAMDROK-TSO

Tibetans have always been proud of their splendid scenery and natural attractions. The Chinese have a developers attitude towards such things which is about a century behind modern thinking. When you drive a few hours out of Lhasa and move from the valley floor up into the mountains you can follow a steep, winding, zig zag, cliff hugging, unsealed road. This two way road is really only wide enough for one vehicle and there is lots of horn blowing from drivers when they come to the blind corners. The coach and truck drivers seem to exercise due caution but there are a growing number of four wheel drive rental vehicles whose drivers appear to be in the Indi 500 Class.

Finally, after negotiating a zillion twists and turns, your brain registers that it is less frightening to focus on the horizon, rather than on the road immediately in front of the coach. When you lift your eyes you can see part of a large industrial project which appears to be on a hilltop in the middle of nowhere.

Then you round one more bend and your breath is completely taken away. Lying below you is one of the most beautiful sights you will ever see on this planet. A totally turquoise lake - Yamdrok-tso. (Tso means lake in Tibetan.) This is one of the sacred lakes of Tibet which mean so much to the local people.

Many of you will have heard of another of the sacred lakes - Lhamo Latso - which is visited by each Dalai Lama as a focus

point for deep meditation. It is said that the future may appear to a Dalai Lama when he gazes into the still surface of the water. These Tibetan lakes in such high altitudes are unique, tranquil and stunning in their clarity and should always be preserved.

However, the Chinese have different plans for Yamdrok-tso. Even though this is a "dead" lake which means it can never replenish its waters once they have been used, the Chinese are draining it for a hydro-electric scheme. I was ashamed to hear some Australians are involved in this abominable project. Surely with our modern technology there is some way around such a destructive act. I feel it is time conservationists started loudly voicing their opposition to this scheme.

How I yearned for the privilege of spending just one night on the hillside overlooking Yamdrok-tso. To be granted a chance to watch as twilight misted its brilliance, to see the moon's glow reflecting from its mirrored surface and to waken at dawn as the morning sky pierced the aqua water with glorious pink and gold beams.

"Farewell Yamdrok-tso. Your demise will bring sadness to many."

Even so, when we look at what the Chinese are planning with the Three Gorges project on the Yangtse River I suppose they would consider criticism of this project in Tibet as a mere hiccup. We met some University students in China (as opposed to Tibet) and when I asked one of them what he wanted to do when he completed his engineering degree he proudly said:

"I hope with all my heart I will be able to work on the Three Gorges project."

There is a real problem when dealing with Tibet when it comes to a matter of protesting issues or providing aid through international agencies and lobby groups. China simply does not recognise Tibet as anything other than an integral part of the Chinese nation. Due to this fact, Tibet is acknowledged as part of China by the United Nations, the World Health Organisation etc. Special assistance cannot be directed to Tibet because it would have to be routed through a major Chinese city. Once this intervention takes place there is no guarantee Tibet would see a penny of the aid. It could end up in the general Chinese coffers. It is incongruous that in this age of modern communications and computers the Chinese still will not co-operate in targeting funding which is only available if it is to be used for a specific project or group of people. China's stance on refusing to direct specific funding for Tibet simply means the citizens of Tibet, whom they like to call Chinese nationals, miss out on much needed assistance.

As the group with whom I travelled were mainly Americans we were granted the privilege of meeting one of their highest political decision makers for the Tibetan region. Along with the Americans I was appalled at the laissez-faire attitude of this man. He told us the Tibetans needed to move into the modern age and the Chinese were ensuring this was happening. He said that young Tibetans were delighted with the changes in their country and welcomed television and modern cars and aerated drinks in cans. He joked that he was being the 'devil's advocate' in the debate but his allegiance to the god of trade and commerce was evident. What he forgot to mention was that this same young generation of Tibetans are still aware enough to remember that their families and friends and neighbours have been tortured and abused by their so-called saviours. His glibness was an insult to all young Tibetans.

His flippant statements annoyed me at the time but mainly because I thought he patronised his fellow countrymen. However, when I returned to Australia I realised just how wide of the benchmark this man had been. In one of our cities there was an exhibition of paintings by children from Dharamsala, which is the Indian home of the Dalai Lama. As these children are the Tibetan exiles I went along expecting to see beautiful paintings of the Tibetan and Indian scenery. Instead, I was nearly physically ill. The eldest of these artists was fifteen and yet they had painted scenes of such torture and horror that adults were reeling as they walked around the gallery.

There were visions of people being burned at the stake, some of them on rotisseries like pigs on a spit. Men had their hands and feet severed and placed in bowls before them. Others were strung upside down from gallows with their heads only inches above flaming fires. There were people in stocks and pillories, some were shackled, others were being shot and tied and whipped and dragged and spat upon.

Never, in my wildest fantasies, could I have pictured scenes of such gross carnage. My senses recoiled and I became angry. But my anger was all skewiff. I went straight up to a Tibetan monk and harangued him.

"I am outraged and appalled," I gasped at him. "This is ludicrous. The Dalai Lama stands for peace and the Tibetans in exile are despoiling their children with such terrible tales that their minds are full of these horrendous scenes. No child should have to listen to stories about this sort of torture. I can't believe what I'm seeing."

The monks eyes welled with compassion.

"You don't realise what has happened in my country do you?"

"Of course I do," I responded. "I've just come back from Tibet but I can't understand why the children in exile are being fed all these horrible images."

"But you really don't understand," he responded gently. "These children are painting what they have seen with their own eyes. No adult is filling their heads with horror stories. They are refugees who have come across the border in recent years. These are not scenes of thirty or forty years ago. They are images which the children have seen since they have been born. As most of them are only just fifteen it means they have seen these ghastly incidents within the past decade, or between the ages of one and five. Their art is a way of expressing their despair at what they have experienced."

My head whirled and my stomach heaved. Nowhere in Tibet

One Stone for Tibet

had I seen the slightest glimpse of the actions behind these abhorrent images. We had just experienced the sterilised "tourists tour" of Tibet.

Certainly we had seen ruins everywhere but the people had never dared to try to tell us what horrors they had seen and endured. What fear they must have of speaking out and sharing their sorrows. Even our drivers and guides who travelled with us for several weeks did not reveal any of their personal stories nor those of any other Tibetans. The few tales we did hear were from European hotel staff or fellow tourists. This was the land of no gossiping about others. We had thought the Tibetans were simply reticent when it came to talking about themselves. Now I understood they probably held secrets which we could never begin to comprehend. How cautious they have learnt to be. How well they conceal the inner depths of their souls from non Buddhists.

No wonder the Chinese are perplexed at the behaviour of the Tibetans. Even if you peel away one layer, they have aspects to their characters about which we can only speculate. My absolute respect goes out to these multi-faceted people who are unique in our world.

There are many sayings concerning "when good men do nothing" and all I can do is say thank you with every fibre of my being to the sterling people around the globe who are now speaking out for Tibet. Thank heavens for the movie stars and their colleagues who are using their energy to create international awareness of the issues.

"Seven Years in Tibet" is a fantastic film and does not shirk from laying it on the line when it comes to the atrocities which have been endured by the Tibetans. Because of the nature of the story my only regret with the film was that it did not have more time to devote to the gentle essence of the Tibetan people who live throughout this wonderful land. It is a bit of a shame the nomadic Tibetans came across as being so fierce because their hospitality is legendary and I would be surprised if they turned a hungry stranger away. Even on re-reading "Seven Years in Tibet" there are many instances of the kindnesses shown to Heinrich and Peter on their journey.

It is true that the Tibetans themselves had to be cautious of some vagabonds and rogues who lived in their own mountains and preyed on all travellers. They will readily admit that there were flaws in their society. However, Tibetans live by the creed of compassion. Sorrel Wilby is an Australian woman who crossed Tibet alone in the 1980's. Her book entitled "Tibet" is a testament to the kindness shown to her by its citizens.

"Kundun" is a movie which manages to dwell more on the uniqueness of the Tibetans as it traces the life of the XIV Dalai Lama until he went into exile in India.

Richard Gere's "Red Corner" is another 'must-see' movie for anyone who is interested in this region.

Finally, although it may not seem to have a bearing on this book, there is another film which I feel compelled to mention. "Field of Dreams" had a profound affect on my life. It gave me the courage to 'give up my day job' to become a full time writer. I thank Kevin Costner and everyone else associated with this film for their vision.

Chapter Fifteen
MILAREPA

Many of us had held a fantasy about Tibet in our hearts before we arrived. Some of us fell totally under the spell of this vast country as we travelled across the barren landscape. At times we travelled for half a day between villages. Several times we joked that the Mars probe had actually photographed Tibet, not the Red Planet itself.

After we left Lhasa we moved up through mountain passes where we could see snow capped peaks all around us. The hillsides were brown and grey rocky slopes dotted with an

occasional scrubby little greenish grey brush. Then the plateau levelled out into a sweeping palette of brown plains as far as the eye could see.

As we approached villages and towns green patches would appear on the horizon and soon we would see the village walls, topped with pats of dried dung. The flat roofed houses which were mostly made of stones and mud bricks were often whitewashed and sometimes painted with coloured stripes which denoted the villagers allegiance to a particular monastery. Donkeys and ponies hauling carts laden with produce would jostle with phenomenal little tractors which looked like a cross between a stretch lawn mower and a motor bike. Yaks and donkeys still pull ploughs but in some villages innovative little hand held ploughs with engines that cough out white clouds of smoke seem to be popular. Usually there were irrigation channels flowing near the towns and one day, when we stopped near a large pond we were surprised to see the surface was iced over. Under bright blue skies we played like a mob of kids as we tossed rocks onto the icy surface in a bid to outdo

Milarepa

each other at distance throwing.

During the day we often only needed a T shirt because of the warmth from the sun, but within hours we could be at an altitude where the wind was so cutting and icy cold that you needed to rug up in down jackets with hoods. When the wind blew over the mountain passes we knew why the Tibetans layered their clothes so effectively.

Any place larger than a village would have the ever present compound for the soldiers. At one small town children ran up to our coach to sell us natural crystals which had been plucked from the surrounding hills. They were doing a roaring trade until the soldiers appeared and then they scuttled across the road and ran to their homes as fast as they could.

If our coach slowed down or stopped children would always rush to greet us with their palms outstretched. Our guide encouraged us not to give them handouts as they were fast becoming accustomed to begging from westerners. Rather, we were encouraged to present any gifts we carried to the local

Milarepa

schoolteacher who could share them fairly. This was very sound advice as, on more than one occasion, we saw petulant little faces when we did not respond to pleas for sweets. We westerners are magnanimous when we travel but we often unconsciously create new social problems in our wake.

Once we stopped on the outskirts of an isolated village and the children who were playing nearby shyly looked across at us. When I tried to take their photo they shielded their faces and peeped at us between their fingers. Finally we were far enough away from civilisation for the manic begging to have ceased!

I must confess. One day I broke the rule. It was a freezing cold day and snow was threatening to fall at any minute. We took a vote and decided we would still stop at the next tiny village because it nestled above Milarepa's Cave. Milarepa was a renowned yogin who lived from 1040 to 1123. In his quest for Nirvana he spent most of his life as a hermit and was a prolific writer of songs and poems. He is renowned for his works including The Hundred Thousand Songs of Milarepa.

As we stopped at the village which was situated halfway down a very sloping hillside, we could see yoked yaks threshing the grain as they walked round and round in monotonous circles. All the adult villagers seemed to be out in the fields and we were soon blessed with several of the local children as guides as we picked our way down the steep pathway to the cave.

We came to a tiny temple jutting out from the hillside but the doors were locked. We couldn't believe we had scrambled all this way for nothing. As we stood and waited at this sacred spot we drank in the view of the valley. Below us the river flowed towards a cleft 'V' between the base of two distant snow capped mountains. Beside the rivers wandering path were villages which looked like toys from this height. I could see a

magnificent eagle flying up this valley. He lived in paradise and Milarepa had certainly chosen well in deciding to spend much of his life in a place of absolute beauty and majesty.

Milarepa would probably have laughed uproariously if he came back today and saw the toilet block next to the temple. This toilet, with its typical holes in the floor framing the view below, was perched hundreds of feet above the valley floor. It had the greatest drop we had yet seen. It was certainly no place for the faint hearted.

A very young monk suddenly appeared and lifted a curtain which nestled against the hillside and we ventured into the cave. It was no more than a couple of very small rooms which were naturally formed within a granite cavern but there was room to stand. We barely had time to take a quick look around as the snow was starting to fall in the valley.

We huffed and puffed as we clambered back up the slope. Two yaks broke through a stone wall above us and blustered across our path. Fortunately they swerved to miss us because we were too exhausted to get out of their way. As we wheezed, heaved and puffed we straggled back to the coach. I was very close to last and as we passed between the walls of two houses where no-one else could see us my little escort turned to me with pleading eyes and held out her hand for a gift. I knew the rules, but she had helped me up and down the path while carrying her baby brother on her back. Deftly I pulled off my warm gloves and slipped them to her as I held my fingers to my lips in the international gesture for silence. She understood immediately, tucked the gloves in her pocket and blessed me with one of the most radiant smiles I have ever seen. We shared a secret and we both knew it.

Chapter Sixteen
GREAT MONASTERIES

Our tour group entered Tibet via Hong Kong and Chengdu in China. After we landed at Gonggar Airport we did not go straight to Lhasa. Instead we travelled through the picturesque Samye Valley to the town of Tsetang which is 180 kilometres south-east of Lhasa. Our guide felt it was too dangerous to move straight into the higher altitude at Lhasa and always preferred to give his groups time to acclimatise. Chengdu was 1,000 ft above sea level and Lhasa 12,000 so we happily accepted his reasoning. This gave us a stepping stone to explore the lovely Yarlung Valley which is a place of rare beauty. The dirt roads are lined with avenues of the most beautiful trees with colours which resemble the gentle greenery of Europe. This was the Tibet of my dreams, a place of enchanting beauty.

From Tsetang we visited Yumbulagang which is reputed to be the oldest building in Tibet. It sits poised on a craggy outcrop which affords panoramic views over the Valley. Sadly, most of the structure had to be rebuilt in 1982 because it was almost destroyed by the invaders in the two decades before.

The ancient Samye Monastery nestles in a tiny sandy delta at the foot of the cleft of a deep valley. This Monastery is held to be the oldest in Tibet and well worth seeing but it is fairly difficult to access. Although it is close to civilisation it is located on the far bank of the Brahmaputra River. The river flows

swiftly and is only navigable by the boatmen who are accustomed to its nuances. It can take a couple of hours to cross a distance which looks swimmable, because the boats have to manoeuvre around shallow patches and counteract currents.

To cross the river there is the option of using coracles which are the famous yak skin boats. These only hold around eight people all of whom need to balance precariously until you can rest your bottom on the struts which support the framework of the boat. You can only put your weight on the cross timber beams because if you put your foot onto the actual yak skin shell you could hole the boat. There was no way any of us were agile enough to manage this manoeuvre for more than a few minutes so after experiencing the thrill of a short ride in a coracle we opted for the more rational choice. We all piled into one of the large open timber boats which look like our little wooden row boats but are ten times bigger. They even use outboards.

We sat or lay down in the bottom of the boat and watched the clouds and felt at peace with the world. We were all rugged up for the journey over the river in the crisp morning air, even with some balaclavas in evidence. By the time of the return journey in the afternoon we had done our classic strip and only wore T shirts again.

From our side of the river the monastery had looked like a little red, green and gold gem which was tantalising us. We soon came down to earth as we had to board cattle trucks for the bumpy ride over rutted dirt tracks to get to our alluring destination.

Samye is a walled enclave with the temple holding pride of place in the centre. The temple is several stories high and from the balconies around the top level you have a panoramic view.

The four corners of the grounds are marked with huge chortens or stupas which are built as acts of merit in Tibet. The outline of a stupa resembles a large onion shaped dome resting on a square base, with a pointed steeple which rises to the sky. There are many variations in shape and size in the Buddhist world and the four at Samye each stood at least fifty feet tall. Sometimes the stupas are only a few feet high, and in other places several stories high. Oftentimes they are used as funerary temples for the ashes of lamas and those of high spiritual merit.

The chortens at Samye were damaged by the Chinese and have just been rebuilt and their garish new paintwork makes them stand out in an incongruous fashion. The main temple is a magnificent emerald green, red and gold. Tibetans believe that the soul of the recently deceased travels first to Samye Monastery.

For all its beauty from a distance and the skill of its design, up close Samye is tired and dirty. The villagers who live around the temple and trade in the few shops seem rather careworn. It is as though the spark has gone out of the community and that is probably very true. Young monks are still in training here with their zealous faces and sunny smiles, but there are very few older monks to lead by example. It appears the place is simply too large for the number of people available to sustain its upkeep. I could imagine it in its heyday when there were hundreds, and at times, thousands of monks, walking the corridors, sweeping the steps, cooking in the cavernous kitchens and generally filling the place with life and vitality. No matter how keen the hearts of the people living there now, the task is simply overwhelming.

When we moved on to Lhasa we were able to visit the world renowned Drepung and Sera Monasteries. These monasteries vary in architecture but both have a very European feel about

them with their magnificent stonework and cobbled streets. They are solid establishments with a masculine feeling about them and they each spread over the lower slopes of a hillside which enables the creation of many interesting nooks and crannies. In both places I felt as though I was on an olde worlde university campus.

Each setting had such wondrous views over Lhasa that it would have been possible to sit in one spot all day and watch as the light changed over the valley below. Samye, in particular, had avenues of softly foliaged trees where you could have rested under a tree in total peace. Both monasteries featured rocks which were brightly painted with images of the Buddha and other deities. Nestled near to Drepung is the dwelling of the State Oracle. We passed nearby but did not have time to visit this special place.

Through the centuries there has been a brotherly rivalry

between the monks in each of these two great monasteries. However, since the Chinese invasion they have bonded into a unified voice. There were times when the Chinese authorities tried to play them off against each other but they soon experienced the folly of this intent.

Each of these monasteries has a little of the ethereal sense of despair which hangs over Samye, but they are better cared for because they are on the main tourist route. Through their very size it is possible to envision how magnificent they must have been in their heyday when they each housed thousands of

monks. Nowadays it is a little like walking on campus when all the students have gone home for a break.

We had a similar feeling in all the monasteries we visited. It was as though the token number of monks were on duty for the day. Occasionally we saw a group of young monks simply chatting in a group but we rarely saw a monk simply sitting in quiet contemplation.

Ganden Monastery is about 100 kilometres north-east of Lhasa but has the most spectacular view of all. Unfortunately this third monastery in the triumvirate of the great monasteries of Lhasa was razed by the communists after they had first trucked all the valuable items back to China. Work is now being carried out to restore the monastery but there is no way the libraries and precious memorabilia can be recreated.

Inside Sera and Drepung the monasteries were similar to the Potala with many magnificent statues and prayer halls. We were privileged to view the simply enormous kitchens where huge brass cauldrons boiled over open fires. If you were a cannibal you could easily have popped six men in each pot. The closest thing I can liken the scene to would be a blacksmiths shop with the naked flames glowing and much of the room covered with the black build up of years of soot. However, on one wall of each kitchen were row upon row of gleaming brass, bronze and copper bowls and jugs. An antique dealer would probably have swooned into a dead faint. Even the butter churns were the height of a man. We could actually see how these kitchens could have supplied meals for thousands of monks a day.

As we explored further even the sanitation arrangements became apparent and these were most impressive. Where the walls hung over the most isolated parts of the grounds below, toilets were constructed. These structures looked like the turrets on the outside walls of medieval castles. You would enter these toilets on the fourth or fifth levels of the monastery. All that was in there was a hole in the stone floor. In an ingenious fashion all

human waste then fell several stories which made it most sanitary up above. At certain times the 'fertiliser' was removed from the lower catchment area and put to good use. We became quite accustomed to these multi-level loos and were much happier using them than many of the other primitive structures which we encountered on our trip.

Our absolute preference was the wide open spaces when we

would dart to opposite sides of the bus. Before we leapt from the bus we would sling our rolls of toilet paper, which we had threaded on to long shoe laces, around our necks. Amidst lots of laughter and several appalling camera opportunities we survived the outback! Fortunately every hotel we stayed in had facilities which came under the headings of great, to barely tolerable but functioning.

Chapter Seventeen
FOUR DIRECTIONS

Our first overnight stop after leaving Lhasa was in Gyantse. The first sight to greet you as you enter town is the old fort on the hill where Francis Younghusband's British troops did a bit of to and froing in the early 1900's. Gyantse once contained fifteen monasteries but now there is only Palkhor Monastery and the incredible Kumbum Chorten. The monastery is traditional but the Chorten is a one off. It rises over four symmetrical floors and is surmounted by a gold dome which sits above the four sets of huge eyes which are painted to face the compass points. Anyone who has visited the Tibetan sector of Kathmandu will be able to picture the impact of the enormous eyes gazing out to the four horizons.

Buddhists are fond of using images to represent concepts and they have also adapted the ancient symbol of the swastika to represent the four directions or the four winds, and by implication the universality of Buddhism. As we are all aware, Hitler perverted the swastika by reversing the image and using it as the Nazi symbol. However, its origins are believed by many to lie in ancient Egypt or even further back where its original meaning has been lost in time. Swastikas are found throughout eastern countries and some can still be found tucked away in Tibet. We came across one particularly stunning image set in turquoise stones in a temple entrance.

One Stone for Tibet

There are many chapels inside the Chorten and you follow a clockwise route as you view them. The walls are all covered with murals and you begin to glaze over after a while and hurry to reach the single chapel at the top where you peep through latticework to take in a panoramic view of the town.

Gyantse itself seems to have a new section and an old Tibetan Quarter. The people appear to be accustomed to tourists and are quite welcoming. We were particularly grateful to the kind gentleman who lifted a fallen electric wire up with a timber pole so our coach could pass safely underneath as we drove down the main street.

Gyantse is no teaming metropolis and the entire town seems to be encompassed within the precincts of two intersecting roads. Within minutes you are out of town and in the midst of pastoral scenes. We were on the road again and heading further across the vast Tibetan Plateau.

On the plateau you are out in the "wide open spaces". By a strange quirk of nature you have no concept of the altitude and there is no way of determining how high you are. At times you cannot even see mountains on the distant horizons. You could just as easily be travelling along a country road at close to sea level.

In reality, of course, because of modern instruments, we knew we were on top of the world. There was simply a lot more 'terra firma' under our feet than when we had been at sea level in Hong Kong. No wonder there are mysterious tales of legendary networks of caves under Tibet. There is lots of earth in which to tunnel.

Chapter Eighteen
PANCHEN LAMA

Shigatse, the second largest town in Tibet is also the home base of the second most important spiritual leader in the country, the Panchen Lama. The Panchen Lamas have always been linked to the Tashilhunpo Monastery.

When the Tenth Panchen Lama was still a child the Chinese rulers whisked him out of Tibet and educated him in China. Their ploy was to raise him as a good communist and play him off against the XIV Dalai Lama by presenting him as the rightful leader of Tibet. However, in 1964 they relieved him of his office and put him under house arrest in Peking as a traitor. They alone knew the reasoning behind this act but they kept him imprisoned for ten years.

As time went on, and Mao died in 1976, the Chinese decided to reactivate their plan to oust the Dalai Lama as the supreme ruler of Tibet. In 1982 they brought the Panchen Lama back into Tibet after keeping him in China for nineteen years. They were confident he would denounce the Dalai Lama. The Tibetan people were delirious with joy to see the Panchen Lama. They flocked to hear him speak and were thrilled to hear him say that he would exercise his office only under the superior authority of the Dalai Lama, whose wisdom and ascetic life plainly predestined him for that high function. The Chinese were left gasping. Their plan had gone horribly awry.

One Stone for Tibet

The Tenth Panchen Lama died of a suspected heart attack when he was back at Tashilhunpo in 1989. Within a couple of years of his death the Tibetans knew it was time to begin the search for the child who would one day become the Eleventh Panchen Lama.

Shigatse is a crossroads town and the hub of much activity. The centre of town seems rather tired and in need of an injection of tender loving care. A couple of street sweepers and a few green parks would have transformed the place. There are no tall buildings in this country setting and the most imposing building is still the magnificent Tashilhunpo Monastery.

When we visited Tashilhunpo it was a festival day. The large courtyard where the dancers were to perform was covered with huge white calico awnings which were embroidered in blue with sacred Tibetan symbols. The four sided courtyard had a stage for dignitaries at one end. At the opposite end were the local people sitting in the fresh air and sunshine as they waited to enjoy the performances by the monks. On either side were covered areas with seating. On one side the monks from the monastery were sitting in tiered rows. On the other side were the 'guests'. The guests consisted of very well dressed Chinese and Tibetan families who were obviously related to the dignitaries on stage, and the not so well dressed western tourists who were travelling through the town

You could almost have imagined this picture postcard scene to be the setting for a day of real rejoicing. That is, until you looked across towards the VIP's. Framed in the colourful archways of the temple stage were dour looking middle aged and elderly men clad in grey and green suits. Several of the men were Chinese, others had Tibetan features but were obviously part of the inner echelon.

Then a most interesting thing occurred. Several robed monks took their places on the other side of the main platform. Seated between them was a tiny little monk of no more than seven years. Our brains went into overdrive. We wondered if this might be the child chosen by the Chinese as their own 'recognised reincarnation of the Panchen Lama'.

We were all aware that this may be the child at the centre of the amazing controversy of 1995.

In 1995 the present Fourteenth Dalai Lama recognised a little six year old boy known as Gandun Chokyi Nyima as the reincarnation of the Tenth Panchen Lama. To the total horror of all pro-Tibetans, the Chinese authorities kidnapped this chosen child and his family, and took them back into China proper. After this dastardly action the Chinese announced that they had found their 'own reincarnation' who just happened to be the son of two members of the Tibetan Communist Party.

Despite the outcry from the Tibetans in exile the Chinese stood by their decision. The European Parliament even passed a resolution of condemnation against China but it had no effect. To this day the Chinese say their chosen child will assume the role of the Eleventh Panchen Lama when he reaches adulthood.

Perhaps this was the boy we saw, perhaps not. Maybe the Chinese have also taken their chosen child into China to be educated. However, the possibility remained. We were certainly in the right monastery in the right city. The little boy before us had such a sweet face. He laughed at the antics of the clowns who entertained the crowd and sat with quiet dignity while the dancers performed. Sadly, we can predict that whoever the little boy is whom the Chinese have chosen, and wherever he is raised, he will face an adulthood of immense difficulty as he

tries to reconcile his pathway with that of the traditional role of the Panchen Lama.

The ceremony began with a slow procession of monks in various colourful costumes. When they reached centre stage they formed two lines facing each other. It was at this point that the silver and gold Tibetan horns were lowered by two monks until one end touched the ground. These horns, which are similar in shape to an Alpine horn, were at least fifteen feet long and when they were played the haunting sound echoed through the still afternoon air. It was a sound reminiscent of the throbbing resonance of the Australian didgeridoo.

The Tibetan dancing was mostly ceremonial and slow but each dance obviously held a significance for the local people. After the first item of entertainment the dignitaries walked down

from the podium to receive khatas from the dancers. There was much merriment when the jesters pretended to steal the white scarves from the community leaders.

The people of Shigatse have seen many atrocities and one of the hardest to bear must have been the destruction of the building which was a second Potala. There are only artists impressions to remind us that this building, which was almost a replica of the Potala in appearance and size, had ever graced the hillside. Our hotel dining room had a wall mural of the layout of the town before the Chinese invasion.

We were really happy to be able to tour the Tashilhunpo Monastery because it has been restored to a reasonable condition. Tashilhunpo means 'Heap of Glory' and from the size of the buildings it is easy to see how the name must once have been entirely appropriate. However, the monks here were the least welcoming and did not seem very keen on seeing tourists. Then again, maybe all the happy monks were off at the dancing and we were left with the ones who had been 'grounded' for the day.

Once again we were in beautiful chapels and enormous grand halls. Once again the dearth of monks going about their daily tasks left us in a type of vacuum. It's all a bit like taking a grand tour of a mausoleum.

We saw the wonderful 86 foot tall Maitreya Buddha statue, and paid dearly for the privilege of taking a photo. I don't suppose Buddha included 'cash collecting' in his teachings, but it has certainly become a large part of the life of a modern monk in Tibet.

Chapter Nineteen
MOVING ALONG

We tended to meander our way across the countryside and often popped onto side tracks which looked like they were heading to nowhere. It was always a revelation, when after seeming hours of bouncing along on the dirt, we would come to a haven which was simply not visible from the main road.

The ancient monastery of Shalu was tucked away at what seemed to be the end of an almost dry creek bed. We had known we were heading somewhere because there was a single telephone line running along the side of the track. It was a quaint sight because the poles supporting the wire were made of clay. We were a long way from any timber!

When we rounded a bend the monastery was tucked in a very cosy spot. Although it is only a small monastery Shalu was renowned as a centre of scholarly learning and psychic training. It was also famous for its ancient and beautiful murals but very few of them remain. I don't think this monastery had electricity as we could only view the murals by candle and torchlight. There were some lovely little corners in this place where the elderly monks greeted us with gentle charm and a little white kitten skipped happily around the sleeping dogs. At last we sensed we were somewhere where the monks were living in harmony with their world.

We were fortunate to meet two elderly Rinpoches on our travels.

One Stone for Tibet

The title Rinpoche is bestowed on highly esteemed and revered lamas. Some Rinpoches receive their title because they are recognised reincarnations. Each of these gentlemen was nearing the end of his life on the earthly plane. They had wizened old faces and gentle compassionate smiles. Only they knew what suffering they had seen in this lifetime. They sat in the lotus position and as we knelt before them and touched our foreheads to theirs, they placed white khatas around our necks. We were asked where we had each travelled from to find our way to Tibet. As they nodded in understanding at the translation of each place name we sensed an unvoiced plea from these wise old men. Were they holding a hope that we may go back to the west and tell the story of Tibet?

The only time we ever felt the Tibetans were aware of the nature of the western world was when we were in the presence of certain lamas and nuns. From one or two of them we felt that they knew that westerners may have the potential to be the source of a glimmer of hope in a land which needs to be healed. The fact that they appeared to know that we were not their enemies was a relief after all the communist brainwashing which they have endured.

Fortunately there are still a few old timers in Tibet who can recall their earlier education. Most monks were once familiar with tales of India and the systems in place in that country because of the constant interaction between the two nations. Many also knew what was also happening in the rest of the world beyond the Tibetan borders. Once these ideas are in a man's head they cannot be taken away with any amount of torture and for as long as that man lives and can speak he can pass on his knowledge.

There were also many lay Tibetans who received well rounded educations prior to 1950. However, we were in no position to meet any of them. These elderly survivors probably still try to analyse the world situation from the limited sources which are available. Presumably, they have learnt to keep their counsel and not trust their innermost thoughts to tourists who flit in and out of their country like butterflies. We westerners tend towards egocentricity and I always imagined that the Tibetans would be desperate to take us into their confidence. However, the lay Tibetan citizens give nothing away in their words or demeanour. Maybe some of them do look to westerners with a glimmer of hope but it is not very likely and certainly not evident. Their only hope is for the return of the Dalai Lama.

For nearly fifty years the Chinese have screened all accessible written material in Tibet. They have told the Tibetans over and over again that America and Britain are enemies of Tibet. The younger generations of Tibetans have no reason to trust westerners. We have shown no evidence of our magnanimity in their world.

A few Tibetan families probably receive news from their relatives and friends in exile but words are not actions. No

One Stone for Tibet

matter how grand our prose and promises to those within the Tibetan borders we have taken no action and given no indication to them of our ability to come to their aid. They are not free to travel to see us, and by doing so to comprehend that our hearts are in the right place and we really do care about their plight.

I am not saying we should use aggression against the Chinese to prove that we care, as that would be abhorrent to His Holiness. All I am saying is that the majority of the younger generation in Tibet today do not know much about the west. Some of them will have heard tales passed down by their elders, but even these stories become distorted with time. There would be very few citizens left in Tibet today who have ever travelled outside its borders. The Chinese have been in control for almost fifty years. The only trips allowed outside Tibet would be into the area which we recognise as the true China.

It is highly likely that the only impressions of the west which are absorbed by the young people are the images which appear on television and the items in the newspapers. There is not much doubt that all media in Tibet is subject to Chinese censorship.

Chapter Twenty
SKY BURIAL

One of my fondest memories of all the monasteries is of the dozing dogs. Every holy place we visited had dogs lolling about in the sun and shade. I had heard tales of vicious packs of dogs roaming the streets at night but I doubt if they came from the lackadaisical ranks of the temple dogs.

Admittedly, when we stayed in Shigatse the dogs would start barking in the wee small hours and not stop until the sun was well over the horizon. I presume this is a habit which was never nipped in the bud and now it is part of the atmosphere of the town. Of course, if you are a light sleeper and not particularly fond of dogs, the experience can send you bonkers.

As we travelled along the Friendship Highway and moved further away from civilisation the conditions became more

trying and it was at this point of our trip that some people began to suffer from a form of debilitating exhaustion which is aggravated by the altitude. This is the sort of feeling which is best alleviated by your own bed at home. However, there is no turning back once you set out across the vast distances in Tibet. There are no helicopters or charter planes to be summoned to rescue you, even if you have pockets full of money. You are in for the long haul and it is a journey which saves the worst till last if you head from Lhasa to Kathmandu. We were slowly broken in to this fact and by the end of the journey we realised our guide had not been kidding around with his warnings.

Many times we wondered at the shock it would be to the system if you came into Tibet from Kathmandu on your way to Lhasa by road. The sudden change in conditions as you crossed the border would certainly make you wonder what sort of a primitive place you were going to find at the end of your journey. The good part would be that you would start off fresh when enduring the worst and from then on conditions only get better travelling in that direction.

We were in a land where we were seeing new sights and discovering new concepts on a daily basis.

By necessity civilisations need to adapt to their surroundings and the Tibetans have learnt to live in harmony with their severe natural environment. This adaptability has led to the ritual of sky burials where the body of a dead person is broken up and offered to the birds. To westerners it may appear as a contradiction in terms to be buried in the sky but it is a matter of using our language to describe something for which we have no adequate word.

In Tibet there are certain special rocks where sky burials are conducted. A dead body is taken to the site and ceremonies are performed in which the body is prepared to be taken by the large predatory birds. The birds are aware of the rituals and do not swoop on the body parts until they are called to take the person back to the realms of nature.

I find this method of disposing of a body particularly sensible and the essence of the idea appeals to me far more than our western traditions. I admire the concept of being a continuing part of the chain of life. It suits my personal belief system. In a similar vein, I am quite content for anyone to have any of my body parts once I'm dead. I can't see that I'll have any use for them!

During our stay in Tibet I actually wrote a new Will. It stated that if I died whilst in Tibet I would prefer a sky burial. I sought permission from the Tibetans to carry out my wishes unless it offended them in any way. Our guide assured me they would generously accommodate my request. I found this a lovely assurance as many cultures would not be as accepting of an outsider intruding into their ceremonies. As we crossed the border from Tibet and entered Nepal the first words my travelling companion said were:

"Thank heavens I didn't have to carry out your wishes! That Will is now invalid and I won't have to explain to your family that I had no body to bring back because you were flying around the Himalayas inside a flock of buzzards tummies."

There were a few times on this journey when we saw the powerful birds who live in the grand setting of the mountain ranges. We were all mesmerised one day when we had stepped out of the coach to take photos of what felt like a "hidden" valley. Ranged around us in a splendid circle were the snow capped peaks of many mountains and all of our emotions were uplifted by this isolated place. Then he appeared, sweeping down the valley with his mighty wings outspread. We all gasped as this enormous eagle flew directly over us. He reached the end of the valley and retraced his pathway through the sky until he again swept above us. He took our breath and our words away and left us with a lifetime memory.

Chapter Twenty-One
FORMER GLORY

Anyone seeking isolation need look no further than Sakya Monastery. It is literally hidden away in a valley way way off the beaten track. Wouldn't you know it though, the Chinese found it and there is an enormous scar across the hillside where part of the monastery once stood. It is as though a giant sliced the side off the hill with a huge scalpel. They must have blown the monastery away because all that is left is a smooth rockface.

What remains of Sakya is an ancient fortress like complex where the buildings are designed in a medieval Mongolian style. This ancient place was once the capital of all Tibet and somehow the structures convey this message. There is a grandness in Sakya which is crying out to be restored to its former glory. Here alone we came across an old and mesmerising style of portal. Hanging from the beams were the taxidermied bodies of animals which seemed to have been strung there to ward off danger.

Former Glory

In Sakya we were blessed to meet with the Abbot who delighted us with gifts of fine strips of red cloth which we were to wear knotted around our necks until they fell away. We gathered this was an even more symbolic gesture than receiving a khata from this elderly gentleman. I recalled Shirley Maclaine's account of being given a similar saffron coloured strip of cloth when she visited a lama high up on a mountain top in Bhutan more than twenty years ago.

We nearly caused a minor riot in Sakya through an oversight. The hotel we had stayed in the previous night had supplied box lunches for our trip to Sakya. We were given permission to sit on the courtyard steps while we ate our lunch. This was all fine, but somehow two western magazines were carried in to the monastery in the carton which held the lunches. There were several teenage monks chatting to our group and when they saw the magazines they pounced on them and began to flick through the pages with obvious glee. Their faces were a delight to watch as they giggled and pointed at the pages. Fortunately one was Time magazine and the other was Tattler so there was not much leeway for the corruption of minors.

We were bemused to see that most of the young monks here wore cheap western watches and sneakers. That was certainly a break with tradition for in earlier times monks were not allowed to wear jewellery. Although their monastery was isolated, these lamas were quite close enough to the Nepalese border for traders to procure goods from the outside world. We found the young monks most willing to communicate and pose for photos. They were more than happy to lead us through several of the shrine rooms which were adorned with brilliant jewel colours. We saw our first sand mandala here and gazed in wonder at shelves of books which reached to the ceiling.

This monastery evidently has strong links with an exiled family who live in America. One day I can see there will be strange times when some of the many Tibetan children who have been born in exile are given the chance to visit the land of their ancestors. Sakya, in particular, feels desperately isolated from civilisation as it is perceived in America. I think it is partly because the monastery itself dominates the town with its massive grey facade. It is the only monastery which seemed, by its design, to block out the outside world. It created a sense of "them and us". Sakya appears to have been built to keep out invaders, not to enhance worship through the beauty of its design. The structure replicates Incan design, appearing thicker at the bottom and rising to create massive blank walls.

To enter this cloistered world you pass through a huge archway.

Your instant impression is that this gateway would look fantastic with a drawbridge and moat.

Once you are inside the monastery walls there is no intrusion from the outside world. However, there are many sunlit areas which belie the initial impression of austerity. You soon step into a surprisingly pretty, yet rustic courtyard, where brightly painted windows overlook the cobbled square.

When you move back outside the monastery walls in Sakya you feel you are still in a time warp. Little donkeys laden with hay are herded along the dusty riverbank and horses and carts are in the streets. Most of the people live in little settlements dotted beside the road to the monastery. They must struggle hard to eke out a living in this far corner of the Tibetan plateau where there are no trees and hardly a trace of greenery. After a time even the vastness of the stark brown scenery can become stifling in its sameness.

In most places I visited in Tibet I could have happily settled. I adored the sweeping panoramas. The rarefied air suited me admirably. But in Sakya something felt different. Maybe we were tired after our long journey, but it did not feel like that was the cause of the sensations. Somehow I sensed that the spirits had been badly disturbed at Sakya and they were not yet ready to settle peacefully over this scarred land. Something is awaiting completion.

Chapter Twenty-Two
LANDSLIDES

From the time we arrived in Tibet we were made aware of the number of landslides which affect travellers. We were warned that a particularly large slide had occurred near the Nepalese border and may not be cleared before we reached it in a few weeks time. Although we were told about it and offered the option of flying out of Lhasa, none of us really believed the road would still be unpassable by the time we arrived there. We were wrong!

As we crossed more of the landscape we realised we were in a country where nature is virtually untamed. If the elements wish to make a point they go right ahead and do it! Man either adapts or perishes.

At the end of each day we offered silent prayers of thanks for our safe journeys over the treacherous unsealed roads. There were so many times when one lapse of concentration on the part of our driver could have sent our coach sliding off a mountain.

One day we rounded a sharp bend and far below on the valley floor was a crushed Range Rover. Our guide told us it had plunged over the cliff the previous day and two people were killed and one badly injured. He told us it was fortunate those killed were local people because if a tourist dies it means the closure of the tour operator's business. Tibet is certainly a land to be traversed in daylight.

The day we saw the north face of Mount Everest on the horizon we knew we were nearing the end of our journey. We stood outside the coach in biting icy cold winds, with the sounds of prayer flags whipping in the air around us, and snapped our photos of this mighty mountain which has claimed the lives of so many adventurous souls. Through binoculars we could actually see two tiny figures, one in red and the other in blue, as they pitched themselves against the elements on the icy slopes.

Although the other mountain slopes were bathed in sunshine and looked relatively peaceful, there was a mighty wind gusting down the higher peaks of Everest and sending enormous drifts of snow into the clear sky. The mountain appeared to be issuing a challenge to any who dared to climb her slopes. Come close to me and I will test you.

We were surprised that Everest is a seemingly chunky mountain when viewed against its neighbours. It does not soar into a majestic peak, but rather, appears massive and bulky. Even when we later flew up the valley in Kathmandu to view Everest

from the other side it had the same appearance of solidity. On that day, it alone of all the mountains had a ring of cloud cover below its summit. It was easy to distinguish because the clouds were evidence that it was the highest mountain in the chain.

We were moving closer to the Nepalese border and coming down from the Tibetan plateau. For the first time in weeks we were passing scrubland and then we moved into tree lined valleys with awe inspiring panoramas. Waterfalls spilled down every hillside from enormous heights. They eroded the slopes and there were many times when we passed small landslides which encroached on the dirt road which wound round the twists and turns of the valleys. Several times the 'main' road crossed through shallow swiftly flowing fords and our coach driver received due applause each time we made it through one of these rocky riverbeds.

It had been snowing lightly and now it began to drizzle. We tried to

One Stone for Tibet

take photos to show how scary it was as our coach rounded a series of S bends where the drop over the side was hundreds of feet to the swiftly flowing river below. Even though we had been on dangerous roads for most of the trip this was different. This time the surface of the road was like ice, the valley was overcast and dull and we held our breath every time another vehicle appeared because there simply didn't seem to be enough room for them to move past.

Then we stopped. We peered through the windscreen wipers to see the reason and there was a weird scene before our eyes. We were in a queue. In front of us were several cattle trucks, which

were used to transport everything in Tibet, including people. There was one coach which we recognised as belonging to an Austrian tour group who had been a little ahead of us but there was no-one on board.

"This is it!" our tour leader cheerfully called out. "We're at the landslide and it's still not open to large vehicles so we have to pick up our

Landslides

handluggage and walk across. There are plenty of porters to carry our larger luggage."

Plenty of porters was an understatement. As we stepped down from our coach we could see there was a whole nomadic village set up on the lower side of the landslide. Tents were propped on every available bit of non-sloping land, and that basically meant they were on the side of the original road. One false step and there wasn't much to stop you tumbling to the bottom of the valley.

Sherpas appeared from everywhere and offered to carry our bits and pieces. This was real capitalism. Any vehicle larger than a sedan could not pass this spot because the landslide had left a huge overhang of rock which would tear the tray off a cattle truck or the roof off a coach. So, these enterprising fellows were willing to walk across what was left of the pass with whatever load needed to get through.

By this time we all cheered up at the prospect of a real adventure and gingerly began to make our way across the narrow trail. A whole section of the hillside had simply come down and taken most of the road with it. In one section the Sherpas had placed several large logs over a nasty gap in what little was left of the road. This was the bit where we chose not to look down but when we considered the men up here were crossing this spot many times a day we had to laugh at the egocentricity which makes us think the whole thing is going to collapse just as we set foot on it.

There were whole families camped at the site until the maintenance work was completed. As we peeped into their makeshift tents women were cooking, feeding babies and making sure their little ones did not fall off the mountain.

We learnt that drivers of the trucks and coaches would execute

Landslides

many pointed turns on this narrow track until they could turn their vehicles around to go back the way they had come.

Our guide cheerfully told us we would be able to hitch a lift on one of the many cattle trucks which were waiting to pick up a paying load before they moved away. We certainly weren't stranded. This transient camp was a metropolis against some of the places we had been. It's just that our options were looking decidedly rough.

We had already been on one cattle truck when we visited Samye Monastery and I must admit the thought of travelling on another while it was still drizzling was not a scintillating prospect.

Suddenly good old reliable Pasang-la called out.

"Relax everybody. Another coach is on its way to pick us up."

Now we knew none of us had walkie-talkies and we all peered down the valley in vain hope of seeing the coach. Meanwhile, every available cattle truck driver on the lower side of the landslide was frantically trying to convince us that his truck was the best on the mountain for our downward journey.

Lo and behold about fifteen minutes later a coach rounded the last bend on the rise before the build up of cattle trucks. The Austrian tour group had fluked this coach earlier and had sent it back for us. Pasang-la smiled knowingly and told us how he had seen a white dot in the distance and simply knew it was a coach for us! Were we ever happy to get out of the rain and continue our journey down the mountain in comfort. To have spent two hours on the back of a cattle truck as it pitched downhill in the rain may have been the undoing of most of us.

Chapter Twenty-Three
WELCOME AND FAREWELL

Accommodation in Tibet is an interesting experience because most of the hotels which are recommended as stopover points for tourists are controlled by the government. We were most fortunate when we were in Lhasa as we stayed at the Holiday Inn which was jointly managed by the hotel chain and the government. However, soon after we left the hotel the last of the European staff moved out of Lhasa. Evidently the logistical problems of joint control became overwhelming. The Holiday Inn boasted several great restaurants but the most famous was the plagiarised "Hard Yak Cafe" with a Yak's head mounted on the wall.

We only had one disturbing moment during our stay at the Holiday Inn and that had nothing to do with the hotel itself. We had risen at dawn because we needed an early start. As I was standing at the window watching the mist lifting off the

hillside I recoiled at the sound of three quick gunshots. Could it have been a car backfiring?

We were soon enlightened when we went down to breakfast. One of the staff members told us quite calmly that we had heard the shots of a firing squad carrying out an execution. They had become quite accustomed to this practice and accepted it as normal.

On our tour we followed the Friendship Highway from Lhasa to Kathmandu and sampled the delights of bureaucratic management. On one occasion we were all in the coach awaiting the all clear to depart a hotel where we had stayed overnight. The next thing our tour leader jumped on board and singled out one of the doctors in our group.

"Doctor," he announced. "Is it true you cracked the toilet seat last night?"

"Why yes," the guilty party responded. "How did you know?"

"It's quite simple. The walls have eyes and ears and we can't leave until you pay twenty dollars!"

"Twenty dollars for a cheap piece of plastic!"

"That's the price and we're stuck here until it's paid."

Amidst a great deal of good humoured bantering the doctor stepped off the bus to pay the fine. We all laughed in delight at such absurdity as we drove on to the next night's stopover point.

Then, the very next morning it was my turn.

We were all on the coach again waiting for our leader.

"Well Janice, you're the criminal today. You broke a plastic coathanger last night didn't you?"

"My God. I am guilty but how did they find out? We were

staying on the third floor and we actually hid the evidence in a rubbish bin in the lobby."

The entire group roared with laughter at my endeavour to carry out the perfect crime.

I had a picture in my mind of maids running into the rooms, each armed with an abacus. I could see the frantic adding up of every cake of soap and every thin faded hand towel.

This time we could not leave until I had paid five dollars for the coat hanger. Plastic is obviously very expensive in the mountains! My payment was more than a month's salary for a hotel worker.

The further we travelled from Lhasa the more basic the hotels became. They were invariably designed in the style of early American motels with a central lobby and restaurant area and then rectangular wings which contained rectangular rooms. In a country where architecture was an evident skill, these fabricated eyesores are a blot on the landscape.

Many of the rooms have recently been renovated to accommodate Chinese officials who are obviously demanding better conditions as they move freely about the countryside. However, as we moved further off the beaten track we came across a couple of 'horror' hotels. One was so far from civilisation that the staff were drawn from the local nomads if and when they were around. We were told the sheets could well have been on the beds for weeks and after one glance at them, which confirmed this belief, we slept on top of the beds. It was freezing cold but at least we weren't out in the elements.

There was one consolation at this hotel. In the middle of the night we scrambled up a flight of stairs onto the roof. We were in the midst of true darkness There were no villages in the distance with glowing lights which could distort our view. The stars, set against a backdrop of black velvet, were dripping their brilliance onto our upturned faces. Putrid sheets meant nothing when we gazed at the miracle in the heavens above.

Our very last hotel before we left Tibet was another gem. This was in a town set against a hillside slope where humanity spilled onto the street at all hours. Some of our group who unluckily scored the front rooms in the house were kept awake by flashing neons, bar brawls and pimps and prostitutes fighting outside their windows. This was in addition to any species of indeterminate origin which may have chosen to cross the floor under cover of darkness. Oh no, we were back into civilisation!

The next morning we rose at dawn in an attempt to be the first in the queue at the border crossing. One of our ladies on the tour had been really ill for two days and we needed to get her into Nepal as soon as we could. She was incapable of walking and our guide had managed to hire a small sedan for her before we came to the landslide so she had been driven across this

hazard. Fortunately she was lying down when the car negotiated the track or she may well have had a coronary on the spot!

The Austrian group joined us at the Passport window a little later and laughed at our ability to hit the road ahead of them for once.

After a tedious process our passports were all stamped and we were ready to head down the valley to the Friendship Bridge which marked the true border. The Austrians were in a jolly mood and we soon found out why. They had co-opted the only bus in town and they knew it! They chortled with glee as we climbed aboard another cattle truck to carry us over the last six kilometres of Tibetan soil.

As we bounced and rolled down the hillside in the chilly, soggy morning air we realised we were coming to the end of our visit to Tibet. Our guide told us that no-one who visits Tibet ever leaves without profound changes in their thinking. I understand what he means. I have watched people change when they interact with dolphins. In Tibet we felt ourselves changing in the same mystical way. You can't put it into words, yet you know it is happening.

One Stone for Tibet

As we crossed the bridge into Nepal we waved goodbye to our Tibetan friends who had been with us on our trip. They had cared for us and nurtured us in so many ways. Most of all, they had been constantly cheerful companions who were delighted to share their magnificent country with us. We knew that they each had their sorrows from living under the communist regime, but they never sought to burden us with their cares. Some of us longed to know their sorrows but they are a gentle and private people who believe suffering is to be born, not railed against.

A sparkling coach awaited us on the other side of the river. One more passport check and we were on our way.

Within two miles of the border I was appalled by a simple incident. We had been told that there were many people in these border towns who would report anyone they suspected may have illegally escaped from Tibet. We could not believe people would do this to their fellow men when they knew the reasons why people seek to become refugees.

We were stopped at a checkpoint which was a simple bamboo pole lowered over the road at the entrance to a tiny village. The Nepalese authorities were checking our papers. As we waited small children ran up to our coach and begged for sweets at the windows. I called out a greeting to a dear little boy of only three or four who stood under my window. It was the Tibetan equivalent of the Hawaiin "Aloha".

"Tashideleg," I called to him as I greeted him with a wide smile.

His little face scrunched up into a grotesque grimace and he literally spat at me. He followed this horrible deed with a yell:

"No tashideleg," he screamed. "No tashideleg."

Those of us who witnessed his actions were stunned beyond belief. There was so much hatred in his little face. Hatred which could only have been put there by the adults in his life. It was so sad that this tiny child had been taught to hate the Tibetans and their country was less than ten miles away from where he lived.

As we followed the switchback trail down the mountainside into the lushness of Nepal a strange lethargy overcame us. The warm, moist air felt oppressive after the crisp rarefied air of Tibet. As we drove through some of the most beautiful scenery imaginable we were all quiet for probably the first time since we had set out. A melancholia had settled over us. We had all been on a journey of a lifetime and many of us wanted to turn right around and do it again. We were like a mob of kids who were being dragged back to school when we wanted to stay on holiday. We had simply loved being in Tibet. The Chinese had tried their hardest to destroy all traces of Tibetan culture but enough remained for us to feel the essence of what had been.

We all longed for a world where the leaders had enough guts to stand up to the Chinese and say:

"Enough is enough! You've decimated this precious land and its people and now it is time to say you're sorry and move out of Tibet. Show the world the greatness which China used to display. The greatness of a nation which once led the world in culture and wisdom. Be astute enough to admit that South-East Asia may only prosper if Tibetans are once again allowed to become the "guardians" of the precious land at the top of the world."

We had heavy hearts as we realised the enormity of persuading the Chinese to do an about turn. However, we live in a world where miracles still occur. One strong Chinese leader with a visionary outlook is all it need take.

Our "One Stone for Tibet" in this century has been His Holiness with his unwavering compassion and focussed peaceful purpose which has raised awareness around the globe.

My prayer is that in the next century the "One Stone for Tibet" is a Chinese youngster who is already born and waiting in the wings to facilitate one of the greatest humanitarian gestures seen on this planet.

Be kind to all children. One child may hold the key to Tibet's future.

Later in the day we arrived at the Holiday Inn in Kathmandu and felt we had spanned centuries, rather than miles. Marbled opulence awaited us. We had crossed a border and were back in a land where five star living could be purchased with a piece of plastic.

EPILOGUE

I am the sort of traveller who is a travel agents dream. When I decide to go somewhere it is usually because I have an inner yearning that I "must" see a particular country and just need to get there somehow. Generally I don't know much at all about the place until I arrive. At times I have come home only to find I missed some of the best and most interesting sights because I hadn't swotted first.

When we came home from Peru and I realised we had actually flown over the Nazca Lines, at a height too high to see them, I was almost hysterical with rage at my stupidity. For years I had read about these incredible lines across a desert in South America, but of course it didn't enter my head that there was desert in Peru. I don't remember any school geography lessons where we discussed the Atacama Desert. No-one had jogged my brain to remind me that the coast of Peru is home to the driest climate in the world and they are lucky if it rains twice a year. So much for my visions of the Amazon jungle tangling its way down to the sandy beaches.

I am also the woman who visited Peru because I wanted to see the Mayan and Aztec ruins. I was a little surprised, but not at all disappointed to find that Macchu Piccu and all the other fascinating ruins were actually Incan.

The problem with this rather vague methodology is that you really need to take at least two trips to every country. I had to "re-do" Egypt because of a few blunders such as missing the Valley of the Queens because I'd never heard of it!

Therefore, you may understand a little better that I did not really know why I wanted to go to Tibet except that "I had to". I was desperate to see the Potala Palace, but apart from that I was ready to go with the flow.

This lack of preconceived ideas meant that absolutely everything in Tibet was a revelation. I had been to see the Dalai Lama twice when he had come to Australia but I cannot recall ever having been inside a Buddhist Temple. I knew Tibetan monks wore maroon robes, but that hardly meant I was familiar with the culture and customs of this secret land. Along with many others, I was aware that China had annexed Tibet, but this didn't really register in my psyche. I could not picture a land overrun with soldiers.

As we traversed one small part of this enormous land we came to sense the special essence of the Tibetan people. Being Australian I had travelled extensively in South-East Asia as it is a little like our backyard. I had met people of many Asian nationalities and the Tibetans were unique. To me they were certainly not Chinese, although I know that people of Mongolian extraction may be regarded as Chinese.

It was with this sort of muddled background that I began to read up on Tibet once we came home. Nowadays it is simple to access books on any country because a good book store simply prints out a list of hundreds of choices for you to peruse.

I find that reading up on a country once you have been there is really most enjoyable. It enables you to picture things very clearly. The pages seem to come alive when you have a vague idea which side of the Seine is graced by the Eiffel Tower, just how high the Seven Hills of Rome appear to be and if the

Epilogue

statues on Easter Island face inland or out to sea.

After a few weeks and several powerful books it hit me! I had floated through this wondrous land with barely any appreciation of the total devastation which had overtaken the Tibetan people. Certainly I knew that most of the monasteries had been destroyed. We saw evidence of that destruction at every turn. I also knew that the Chinese were simply everywhere in Tibet. I knew the Dalai Lama had fled. I knew people were tortured. But how much did I really know?

As I read Heinrich Harrer's sequel, "Return to Tibet", I began to absorb the immensity of the tragedy which is modern Tibet. Heinrich's words of despair for the nation he had loved and the changes he had witnessed, resonated powerfully. It was decades since I had first read "Seven Years in Tibet", but with this second book his heart was aching for the Tibet which used to be.

I finally read the Dalai Lama's autobiography. Yes, I had been to Tibet without having read this inspirational story. Each tome I picked up came alive in my hands. The experience of having met Tibetan people face to face was helping me to understand the intensity of each of the books I selected. The pieces were falling into place and I was beginning to see why I had been so powerfully drawn to Tibet.

I had been privileged to visit a unique land which is home to a unique race of people. They demand nothing on this earth and give thanks for what they have. I had glimpsed the people who had dwelt in our imaginations in Shangri-la.

They had hosted our trip to their country with innate gentleness. Our guides were very careful not to influence our thinking in any way. They took delight in showing us their land and its people, but they never moaned or whined or even mentioned the fact that the Chinese had turned their lives upside down. These calm and self-effacing people never sought to make us sounding boards for their troubles.

We were left entirely alone to 'read between the lines' of any conflict if we even wished to entertain such thoughts.

I found this quietness about the turmoil almost mystifying. In hindsight, I realise that after many decades of torture and learned caution, the Tibetans are not likely to pour their hearts out to strangers.

Their apparent acceptance of the changes in their country probably reflects their depths of caution in revealing sorrows to those who may betray their trust. A coachload of tourists may appear to be a happy, trustworthy lot, but only a Tibetan would understand how presumed friends have even betrayed each other in the troubled times since the Chinese arrived. The Tibetans have learnt to keep their own counsel and pray secretly for the return of His Holiness to restore peace to their land.

The Tibetans who still reside in their country have no forum which they can trust. They can secretly hope we westerners may speak out on their behalf when we leave their land, but they are neither audacious nor foolish enough to risk sharing their concerns.

The need for a worldwide plea for the Tibetans can only be voiced freely by those who live in democracies. Therefore, it is essential that those of us who enjoy this privilege should make absolute use of it.

I felt an overwhelming urge to write this book. There are many who know more than me about "the top of the world", which means it may contain inaccuracies. If so, I apologise to any

Epilogue

whom I may have offended. It is simply written in the hope that it may inspire you to delve into more books about Tibet and as you learn more that you will share your knowledge with others.
Understanding leads to enlightenment.

Tashideleg.